Technology's challenge to science education

DEVELOPING SCIENCE AND TECHNOLOGY EDUCATION

Series Editor: Brian Woolnough
Department of Educational Studies, University of Oxford

Current titles:

John Eggleston: *Teaching Design and Technology*
David Layton: *Technology's Challenge to Science Education*
Keith Postlethwaite: *Differentiated Science Teaching*
Jon Scaife and Jerry Wellington: *Information Technology in Science and Technology Education*
Joan Solomon: *Teaching Science, Technology and Society*
Clive Sutton: *Words, Science and Learning*

Titles in preparation include:

Michael Poole: *Beliefs and Values in Science Education*
Michael Reiss: *Science Education for a Pluralist Society*

ERRATUM

On page 51 the first paragraph beginning 'The essential point here is . . .' should read:

> The translation of scientific knowledge into a form which articulates with the design parameters in terms of which technological interventions can be made, thus provides a rational basis for the deployment of available resources and the aims of associated health education programmes.

The second paragraph beginning 'The essential point here . . .' is correct as printed.

Technology's challenge to science education

CATHEDRAL, QUARRY OR COMPANY STORE?

DAVID LAYTON

Open University Press
Buckingham · Philadelphia

Open University Press
Celtic Court
22 Ballmoor
Buckingham
MK18 1XW

and
1900 Frost Road, Suite 101
Bristol, PA 19007, USA

First Published 1993

A catalogue record of this book is available from the British Library

Library of Congress Cataloging-in-Publication Data

Layton, David, 1925–
Technology's challenge to science education: cathedral, quarry, or company store?/David Layton.
p. cm. — (Developing science and technology education)
Includes bibliographical references and index.
ISBN 0–335–09959–9. ISBN 0–335–09958–0 (pbk.)
1. Science–Study and teaching. 2. Technology education.
3. Curriculum development–Great Britain. I. Title. II. Series.
Q181.L488 1993
507'.1 – dc20 92–30287
CIP

Typeset by Type Study, Scarborough
Printed in Great Britain by St Edmundsbury Press,
Bury St Edmunds, Suffolk

Contents

Series editor's preface		7
Acknowledgements		9
CHAPTER 1	The emergence of technology as a component of general education	11
CHAPTER 2	Technology in the National Curriculum of England and Wales	17
CHAPTER 3	Understanding technology – 1 The seamless web	23
CHAPTER 4	Understanding technology – 2 Values, gender and reality	31
CHAPTER 5	Science as a resource for technological capability	41
CHAPTER 6	Reworking the school science–technology relationship	57
CHAPTER 7	Responses and resources: a review of the field	67
Index		79

Series editor's preface

It may seem surprising that after three decades of curriculum innovation, and with the increasing provision of a centralised National Curriculum, that it is felt necessary to produce a series of books which encourages teachers and curriculum developers to continue to rethink how science and technology should be taught in schools. But teaching can never be merely the 'delivery' of someone else's 'given' curriculum. It is essentially a personal and professional business in which lively, thinking, enthusiastic teachers continue to analyse their own activities and mediate the curriculum framework to their students. If teachers ever cease to be critical of what they are doing, then their teaching, and their students' learning, will become sterile.

There are still important questions which need to be addressed, questions which remain fundamental but the answers to which may vary according to the social conditions and educational priorities at a particular time.

What is the justification for teaching science and technology in our schools? For educational or vocational reasons? Providing science and technology for all, for future educated citizens, or to provide adequately prepared and motivated students to fulfil the industrial needs of the country? Will the same type of curriculum satisfactorily meet both needs or do we need a differentiated curriculum? In the past it has too readily been assumed that one type of science will meet all needs.

What should be the nature of science and technology in schools? It will need to develop both the methods and the content of the subject, the way a scientist or engineer works and the appropriate knowledge and understanding, but what is the relationship between the two? How does the student's explicit knowledge relate to investigational skill, how important is the student's tacit knowledge? In the past the holistic nature of scientific activity and the importance of affective factors such as commitment and enjoyment have been seriously undervalued in relation to the student's success.

And, of particular concern to this series, what is the relationship between science and technology? In some countries the scientific nature of technology and the technological aspects of science make the subjects a natural continuum. In others the curriculum structures have separated the two leaving the teachers to develop appropriate links. Underlying this series is the belief that science and technology have an important interdependence and thus many of the books will be appropriate to teachers of both science and technology.

Professor Layton's book tackles these issues directly. He asserts that simplistic models of the relationship between technology and science must be rejected, most of which ignore the values and cultural dependence underlying technology. He encourages us to move beyond a view of technology as artefacts and see it as a social phenomenon and expression of human work. Considering the relationship between school science and technology, he asks us to decide between science as a cathedral, a quarry or a company store! His conclusion is that 'the inclusion of technology in the curriculum of general education entails a change in the culture of schools. It is not that the existing culture, with whatever emphasis this might have on academic achievements and pastoral concerns, needs to be replaced. Rather, it requires enhancement by the celebration of practical capability as an extension of scholastic attainments into the wider world of purposeful design and action.'

This is an important, perceptive, scholarly book, which is both analytical and radical. It clarifies many issues, and clears away many myths, which have in the past made the progress of technology in schools so uncertain and of science in schools so reactionary.

We hope that this book, and the series as a whole, will help many teachers to develop their science and technological education in ways that are both satisfying to themselves and stimulating to their students.

Brian E. Woolnough

Acknowledgements

The ideas in this book owe much to discussions I have had over several years with colleagues both in the Centre for Studies in Science and Mathematics Education, University of Leeds, and in other universities in the UK and overseas. They are too numerous to name, but they know who they are and I hope they will accept my thanks for scholarly communion and generosity of intellect.

My involvement in a substantial project of the OECD, involving the analysis of case studies of innovations in science, mathematics and technology education in OECD member countries, has been the source of valued information and insights. Similarly, the opportunity to edit for UNESCO a series of volumes on *Innovations in Science and Technology Education*, drawing on contributions from science and technology educators worldwide, has provided even more inclusive perspectives on the role of technology in general education and the relationship between school science and school technology. It will be clear also that I owe a special debt to the community of historians of technology: at an international conference on Technological Development and Science in the Nineteenth and Twentieth Centuries, held at Eindhoven in 1990, I had the enriching experience of working alongside several of the leading contributors to this field. Their influence is evident throughout the book.

More particularly, my membership of the Secretary of State's National Curriculum Working Group on Design and Technology, chaired by Lady Margaret Parkes, and my subsequent involvement with groups of teachers in England and Wales who were implementing the 1990 Statutory Order for Technology, provided a demanding test bed for ideas on the emerging relationship of school science and school technology. The major part of the book was written before proposals for a revised Order were published in December 1992. It was encouraging to see the restoration of cross-references to the Science Order in that document, although it is the contention in what follows that if science is to fulfil its role as a potent resource for the development of children's technological capability, much more is required than a mere collating of topics from the two Orders. The terms of reference of the group established to revise the 1990 Order included the injunction to 'clarify how and when the skills, knowledge and understanding developed through other Curriculum Orders should be made use of in technology.' With respect to science, this would serve as a description of the purpose of the seven chapters which follow.

A number of curriculum development projects concerned with the relationship between school science and school technology have generously made their published and trial material available to me and I have been able to use this to illustrate some curriculum issues, notably in Chapter 7. Their collaboration is greatly appreciated and attributions are made in the text at the appropriate points.

For permission to reproduce figures and tables, I am indebted to the following: Dr Arnold Pacey and Basil Blackwell Publishers Ltd (Fig. 3.1); *New Scientist* (Table 4.1); The Schools Examinations and Assessment Council (Figs 4.1 and 4.2); The World Bank, Washington (Table 5.2); The Making Use of Science and Technology Project (Figs 7.2 and 7.3); The Science with Technology Project (Fig. 7.4).

I am especially appreciative of the willingness of the Association for Science Education to allow me to reproduce its Policy Statement on Technology, approved by Council in May 1991, as an Appendix to Chapter 7.

Certain passages in the chapters have appeared in, or have been adapted from, work that I have published elsewhere and I am grateful to the editor, Edgar Jenkins, and Studies in Education Ltd, for permission to use material which appeared in volume 19 (1991) of *Studies in Science Education*; The Centre for Studies in Science and Mathematics Education, University of Leeds, for permission to use material which formed a chapter in E. W. Jenkins (ed.) (1990) *Policy Issues and School Science Education*; and The Department of Education, University of Liverpool, for permission to draw upon material published in *Inarticulate Science?* (1990) Occasional Paper No. 17.

CHAPTER 1

The emergence of technology as a component of general education

Influences for change

For teachers wrestling with the everyday problems of school life, striving to do their best for their pupils whilst coping with incessant change imposed from outside, it may not be obvious that a radical transformation of mission is underway. The demands of the immediate and preoccupations with practice deflect attention from the overview.

Yet when an opportunity arises for sights to be raised, it is clear that the goals and contexts of schooling are undergoing major redefinition. Furthermore, this is a general trend in many countries throughout the world. Whilst exploration of the full complexity of these changes lies outside the scope of this book, some indications of the forces driving reform are readily available.

In the UK, for example, a Technical and Vocational Education Initiative (TVEI) for 14- to 18-year olds, after a pilot run of four years, was extended in 1987 to all maintained schools and colleges as a 10-year programme with supporting funds of some £900 million. Significantly, the source of this funding was not the government's Department of Education and Science, responsible for schools, but the Department of Employment. In Australia, this convergence of interests has been acknowledged by the creation of a single Department of Employment, Education and Training. In both these countries, and in others as geographically and economically different as the USA, Finland and Zimbabwe, there are strong movements to encourage work-related or work-oriented learning, linking general education in partnerships with industry and commerce, and reconstructing the interface between vocational and general education. Certainly, any interpretation of vocationalism in terms of a narrow occupationalism or job-specific training is totally inadequate in most contexts today, given the rapidity and pervasiveness of technological change. Successful firms of the future will need workers equipped with 'skills as a general polyvalent resource that can be put to many different and, most importantly, as yet unknown future uses' (Streeck, 1989).

One way of describing these changes is to say that general education is being vocationalised, whilst vocational education is being generalised. To leave matters there, however, would conceal the diverse origins of the impulse for change. The vocationalising of general education is driven by multiple concerns, of which at least five can be distinguished:

1 Economic considerations, both national and individual, have been paramount in many contexts. The opening words of the British government's White Paper entitled *Working Together – Education and Training* (1986, Cmnd. 9823: 1) is typical:

> We live in a world of determined, educated, trained and strongly motivated competitors. The competition they offer has taken more

> and more of our markets – both overseas and here at home.
>
> For the nation and all who work in its businesses – both large and small – survival and success will depend on designing, making and selling goods and services that the customer wants at the time he wants and at a price he is prepared to pay; innovating to improve quality and efficiency; and maintaining an edge over all competition. This will not be just for today or tomorrow but for the foreseeable future.
>
> The same machines and equipment are available to all. Success will go to those (be they firms, communities or nations) whose people can use them to the best advantage. And that requires individual initiative, innovation and competence across the whole spectrum of skills and aptitudes. People – with their knowledge, learning, skills, intelligence, innovation and competence – are our most important asset and resource.

There is a clear message here about the limitations of academic learning and the need for education to articulate more effectively with enterprise in the made-world.

2 A related political concern arises from the prospect that unchanged educational provisions could lead to large numbers of unemployable, disillusioned and alienated young people who would constitute a socially destabilising force. Many pupils in school find meaning and relevance in their studies only to the extent that these are practical and related to the world outside school that they know and understand. A better bridge between school and work is one important aspect of the interpretation of vocationalised general education applied here. For some, also, there is emphasis on the fostering of personal qualities such as reliability, compliance and conscientiousness necessary to ensure an effective and subordinate workforce. Some, at least, of this message is strangely at odds with the requirement for initiative, enterprise and innovation.

3 Recognition of the extraordinary transformatory powers of technological change, not only over the means of production and communication, but also over lifestyles and human values, has brought into prominence a social concern for the control of technology. It is important that we shape it, rather than allowing it to shape us. This entails a crucial critical component in the study and application of technology. One response to this is a critical vocationalism, which goes beyond the acquisition of knowledge and skills for employment, to include an understanding of the context of work in its social, economic, political, moral and aesthetic dimensions (Spours and Young, 1988).

4 In addition to external – economic, political and social – drives for the vocationalising of general education, there are internal educational and epistemological considerations which point in the same direction. The prevailing academicism of much school learning is criticised because it does not equip its recipients for action in what Donald Schön (1987: 6) has called 'the indeterminate zones of practice'. He means by this those all-too-common situations in which decisions are not clear-cut, where the evidential basis for action is uncertain, where probabilities have to be weighed against each other, where constraints on action can be conflicting and unpredictable, and where optimisation rather than irrefutability is a characteristic of solutions. It is argued that, on its own, propositional knowledge, 'knowing that', is not enough; it needs complementing by action knowledge, 'knowing how'. The competencies that distinguish skilful performance in the realms of practical action deserve greater recognition in curriculum terms. Historically, they have had low educational status and have frequently been marginalised in, if not excluded from, the curriculum of general education; 'practical' has been a term of disparagement in contrast to 'academic' or 'scholarly'. The time has now come to redress the balance and 'privilege the practical'.

5 A particular Anglo-Saxon variant of the economic and educational arguments is Martin Wiener's (1981) thesis that schools transmit aristocratic, as opposed to industrial, values, the

emphasis being on the learning, retention and regurgitation of delocalised academic knowledge. It is argued that education in England and Wales has never come to terms with industrialisation, despite the countries being the site of the Industrial Revolution. There is a need to inculcate more favourable attitudes to employment in industry in secondary school students especially. A 'third culture' of technology, incorporated in the curriculum alongside the established 'two cultures' of 'arts' and 'sciences' has been suggested as one way forward.

It will be clear that these various impulses for change contain within themselves the seeds of conflict. For example, a critical vocationalism intended to assist the control of technology might differ in its implications for action from a vocationalism impelled by the unbridled quest for economic competitiveness. It has always been the case, however, that the shaping of the curriculum has depended on the outcome of contests between conflicting interests and so there is nothing new in this situation. Whilst we might expect, and already find, considerable diversity of response, there are, nevertheless, significant common features. Perhaps the most notable of these is the emergence of a new subject, technology, as a curriculum focus for the development of practical capabilities.

The origins of school technology

Unlike school subjects such as chemistry, history and geography, technology does not have a well-established role model in higher education. Representatives of particular technologies are to be found there (e.g. food technology, textile technology) as are the various branches of engineering (civil, chemical, electrical, electronic, mechanical, etc.). In certain countries, there are also higher education institutions where design is taught. However, although attempts have been made to construct general engineering courses, embodying principles common to several branches of engineering, there is no subject called 'technology', comparable to, say, physics or biology. School technology does not have its origins in higher education and the engineering faculties there have not been prominent in urging its inclusion as a component of general education.

What seems to be occurring in many cases is the emergence of school technology from below by a process of subject transformation which differs from country to country. The curriculum ingredients from which the process begins can vary and there is a lack of consensus on the fine details of the end-product. Much depends on the character of the institutions involved and on the precursors of technology which have existed there.

In the USA, for example, many developments in technology education have grown out of the high school curriculum subject called 'industrial arts', itself an evolutionary product of 'manual training'. As the name implies, industrial arts had a content reflective of the different industrial systems such as production, transportation and communication and the processes associated with these. Whilst the American Industrial Arts Association, the professional association of teachers of industrial arts, has now changed its name to the International Technology Education Association, the power of precedent remains strong and much technology education in the USA is still organised around the three systems identified, with the addition of biotechnology as an industrial newcomer. Until comparatively recently, and in contrast to the UK, the process aspects of technology, and the involvement of students in design activities in particular, have received little prominence in the US developments (Todd, 1991).

In the Netherlands, secondary education starts at age twelve and is divided into two tracks, there being both general and vocational schools. Within the vocational schools, a subject called 'general techniques' was introduced in 1973 and has continued there with modifications. A government proposal in 1987 to reform the curriculum of lower secondary education, and to include technology as a subject in both vocational and general schools, led to further developments. Official proposals for the curriculum for technology and for technology attainment targets at 15+ were initially, and perhaps understandably, much influenced by the experiences of teaching general techniques in vocational schools. There was a strong emphasis on the craft skills required for making functional 'work pieces' and little opportunity was provided for pupils to design, as opposed to make and use, technological artefacts. It was stated that 'Not all pupils possess the capability of "providing a solution" to a problem and transforming thought and ideas into concrete form. For most pupils, the design phase will consist primarily of discovering applications' (Attainment Targets Committee for Technology, 1989: 24). Alternative versions of technology education which give more prominence to designing activities, emphasise the learning of general technological concepts and principles, relate technology more strongly to science and mathematics and generally present a more dynamic view of technology, have subsequently been formulated in the Netherlands and are influencing the nature of the reform to some extent.

Finland provides yet another illustration of the recent introduction of technology as a component of general education. In fact, no new subject called 'technology' has been added to the curriculum, but developments have occurred within an existing subject called, since 1975, 'technical work'. The origins of this can be traced back to 'boys' crafts' in the Folk Schools and, later, 'technical crafts' in the Finnish comprehensive schools. Like its precursors – and as its name implies – technical work is intended to relate closely to the prevailing modes of production in the society, although not in a narrow vocational sense. In the recent curriculum developments in Finland, the aim of technology education is to teach pupils to understand and use automation. The emphasis, therefore, is on basic engineering principles, electronics, technical drawing, computer-aided design and manufacture (CAD-CAM) and computer numerical control (CNC). Computer education, initially introduced as a separate subject distinct from technical work, is now being incorporated progressively in all subjects in the curriculum of general education. Within technical work, students have experience of computer-aided design in the production of pieces of work which are machined at numerically controlled work-stations. They experiment with production line simulations, involving robots, assembly lines, measuring equipment for quality control and numerically controlled machines. Computers are used for the control of processes involving motors, relays, solenoids, pumps, etc., and students design automatic processes themselves in project work.

This 'high-tech' and production-orientated version of technology education is in marked contrast to developments in several other countries where a greater emphasis is being placed on the process aspects of designing, making and appraising technological artefacts and systems, and on the cognitive development of pupils in ways which are unique to technology education. The Finnish innovation acknowledges the need to co-ordinate effectively the work that students do in their technical work and in their science lessons, but has encountered problems in this area, not least because of the lack of science in the previous education of the craft teachers who have been retrained for the teaching of technical work.

Without multiplying examples further – and there are comparable and distinctive developments in other countries such as Australia, Ireland, Scotland and Spain, as well as in England and Wales – a number of general points can be made about the origins of school technology and the ways in which it is being incorporated into the curriculum of general education.

First, technology is a new school subject in the sense that it lacks both a history and a tradition as a component of the general education of all children. It is true that in institutions of vocational education, certain branches of technology have been taught, usually in conjunction with the requirements of specific occupations or trades. Typical subjects are automobile technology, building technology, horticulture and cookery. In secondary general education, gender-biased versions for selected groups of students have been common, e.g. woodwork and metalwork for less able boys. The present innovations, however, are different in that most of them are attempting to create a subject which is free of narrow vocational connections and which will extend the most able children while providing experiences of success for those less gifted. There are few reliable benchmarks by which to judge performance; there is as yet no culture of school technology, expressed in common educational beliefs, values, standards and practices, such as is the case with, say, science or mathematics. Indeed, the innovation can be understood as an attempt to create a new culture which places high value on practical capability.

Second, whereas diversity of response seems to be a characteristic of the innovation from an international perspective, this may be more a product of ways of implementing the reform than of deep differences of opinion about what school technology should be. Of course, differences do exist, for example in the emphasis to be given to design activities in the subject, and the situation is not helped by the almost total absence of research into the teaching and learning of technology. Certainly there is no body of research findings on children's learning of technology comparable to that which exists for science and mathematics. This apart, the innovation seems to be characterised in most contexts by a pragmatic approach, accepting the situation which presently exists in precursor subjects, not least with regard to teacher skills and qualifications, and building from this. Because the starting point is so different in the various educational systems, it is not surprising that a snapshot of progress at a relatively early stage of development should reveal diversity. Furthermore, it is understandable that most developments have so far been at secondary school level. That is where the external influences for reform bear more strongly and where subject precursors are more obvious. Increasingly, however, technology is being incorporated in the curriculum of primary schools where the structure of the timetable and the style of working can frequently provide a more hospitable environment for technological activities than is the case in many secondary schools.

Third, a general characteristic of school technology and one which makes it different from many other school subjects is its engagement with practical action in the made world. No subject challenges the historic role of schools as institutions which decontextualise knowledge quite so strongly as does technology. It represents a major revaluation of the kinds of knowledge which a society deems important. Academic knowledge has hitherto been king and, in most subjects, learning has been an end in itself. What technology signals is the recognition that practical knowledge, i.e. knowledge which empowers its possessors in the realms of practical action, is now being accorded equal status.

References

Attainment Targets Committee for Technology (1989) *Proposed Attainment Targets at 15+: Proposals to the Secretary of State for Education and Science in the Netherlands.*

Schön, D. A. (1987) *Educating the Reflective Practitioner*. London: Jossey-Bass.

Spours, K. and Young, M. F. D. (1988) *Beyond Vocationalism*. Working Paper No. 4, New Series. London: Centre for Vocational Studies, Institute of Education, University of London.

Streeck, W. (1989) Skills and the limits of neo-liberalism: The enterprise of the future as a place of learning. *Work, Employment and Society*, 3(1), 89–104.

Todd, R. (1991) The changing face of technology education in the United States. In J. S. Smith (ed.), *Dater 91*, pp. 261–75. Loughborough: Departments of Design and Technology, Loughborough University of Technology.

Wiener, M. (1981) *English Culture and the Decline of the Industrial Spirit 1850–1980*. Cambridge: Cambridge University Press.

CHAPTER 2

Technology in the National Curriculum of England and Wales

Legal framework and subject precursors

The brief sketches in the previous chapter of ways in which technology education is emerging in different educational systems are sufficient to indicate some general features of the innovation. To reveal more clearly the complexity of what can be involved in the construction of a school technology curriculum, however, a more detailed exploration is needed. This will now be undertaken for one development, perhaps the most ambitious attempt so far to incorporate technology as an essential component of general education, i.e. the case of technology in the National Curriculum of England and Wales.

The 1988 Education Reform Act established a minimum entitlement National Curriculum of ten subjects as a legal requirement for all children in state-maintained schools in England and Wales aged 5–16 years. The ten subjects are:

- *Core subjects*: mathematics, English and science;
- *Foundation subjects*: technology, history, geography, music, art, physical education and (for secondary schools) a modern foreign language.

The implementation of the total National Curriculum is a phased process likely to continue throughout the 1990s. Statutory Orders for the three core subjects were published in 1989 and in September of that year the teaching of mathematics, English and science to primary school children aged 5–7 years and of mathematics and science to 11- to 14-year olds commenced. The first of the foundation subjects, technology, was introduced in September 1990 for primary school children aged 5–11 years and for secondary school children aged 11–14 years.

Up to this time, technology had not been a subject of the school curriculum, at least under that name. However, in primary schools, much teaching was thematic, involving cross-curricular approaches and practical activities (e.g. making models) which could contribute to technological capability. In addition, following criticisms that science was being neglected in the primary school curriculum, a greater emphasis had been placed on this subject, much of the work being based on practical technological situations within the experience of young children. What was missing, however, was any attempt to develop technological capability in a deliberate and well-planned progression.

As for the secondary school curriculum, at least six different – and at times competing – strands of activity provided a possible foundation for technology. There was, first, in many schools, still a legacy of craft subjects (e.g. woodwork and metalwork for boys taught by men and sewing and cookery for girls taught by women). These had low status, the courses frequently being restricted to less academically inclined pupils. Few of the men teachers, especially, possessed academic qualifications, their work being categorised as manual rather than mental. It is not surprising that these teachers saw the incorporation of design principles in their work as a way of raising the status of their subjects by adding an apparently cognitive dimension to the making of artefacts.

The teaching of the processes of design, the second precursor of school technology, involved the reconciliation of functional demands (i.e. what was being produced should do what was intended) with the various constraints of the situation (e.g. the limitations of materials available; cost and time restrictions; ergonomic and aesthetic requirements, etc.). This gave intellectual status to the construction of artefacts and systems, and the subject was strongly supported by those urging a greater emphasis on design in industry and in public life generally. The Council of Industrial Design, later the Design Council, was prominent in this field, and successfully recruited the support of influential politicians including Margaret Thatcher when Prime Minister. The boundaries of the subject were not always clear-cut, however, and it was sometimes associated with the teaching of art. From the standpoint of technology, a weakness of the approach was a tendency for pupils' work at the drawing board (and, more recently, at the computer terminal) to predominate at the expense of the acquisition of constructional skills.

A third strand of development, prominent especially in the 1960s and later, and to some extent a reaction to the purity of the science curriculum reforms of this period, involved an attempt to convey to pupils the excitement and challenge of engineering. This was supported by those who wished to encourage more able students to embark upon studies in science and engineering in universities. The topics included electronics, structures, energy transfer, feedback and control, pneumatic systems and even elementary aerodynamics and wind tunnel experiments. There was an emphasis on creativity, as opposed to the allegedly analytical modes of thought associated with the new science curricula. Unhappily, the innovation provoked a conflict over the extent to which craft skills or scientific theory should underpin the work which students undertook. The details of this damaging dispute have been recounted elsewhere (McCulloch *et al.*, 1985; Penfold, 1988) and need not be repeated here. A major national curriculum initiative, 'Project Technology', produced some excellent teaching materials, but, at the time made little impact on the work that was done in the majority of secondary schools.

By the beginning of the 1980s, and drawing on the three precursors above, a school subject known as Craft, Design and Technology (CDT) was appearing in the curriculum of a growing number of secondary schools in England and Wales. This development was strongly supported by some members of Her Majesty's Inspectorate, who had undertaken a review of 'good practice' associated with 'the range of learning that goes on in school workshops' in the 1977–78 academic year (DES, 1980). The attempt to co-ordinate effort in the subject met with some success and helped to raise its status to that of an essential component of general education, the technological area of learning and experience being one of nine prescribed for the curriculum of all schools, both primary and secondary (DES, 1985). Even so, teachers continued to adopt a wide variety of approaches and emphases in their work. Scientific principles, particularly of physics, could be taught by CDT teachers to secondary school pupils who had been taught the same principles, but in a different way, by their physics teachers. Electronics, especially, was a subject which exposed differences in approach. For much CDT work, it was sufficient for pupils to have a functional understanding of devices rather than a fundamental grasp of the underlying physics – knowledge of *what* a transistor could do had priority over *how* it was able to do it.

Within CDT itself, different emphases continued to flourish. When the public examination system at age sixteen was changed in the late 1980s with the introduction of the General Certificate of Secondary Education (GCSE), it was found necessary to provide three different CDT-related examinations: CDT-Design and Realisation, CDT-Technology and CDT-Design and Communication. The extent to which this represents progress is only seen when it is recalled that at the beginning of the decade there were some 1500 different CDT-related examination syllabuses in existence covering fields as diverse as furniture-making, jewellery, rural crafts, motor vehicle studies, geometrical-drawing, control technology and metalwork (Rose, 1988). It was the view of Sir Keith Joseph, Secretary of State for Education, speaking in 1985, that whilst CDT had a vital part to play in a broad and balanced school curriculum and that much had already been done, there was still a long way to go:

> None of us can be satisfied with a situation in which 93 per cent of the subject entries in the CDT areas in public examinations at 16+ are from boys and only 7 per cent from girls, with the imbalance even greater at 18+ and with a situation in which only 2 per cent of CDT teachers are women.
>
> (Joseph, 1985)

As its name indicated, CDT was an attempt to consolidate in one school subject the educational potential of at least three historic and distinguishable strands of curriculum evolution. Alongside this innovation, there were other changes taking place which were seen by their proponents as contributing to an education in technology. The developments in this case, however, came not from craft and design but from science.

A widespread perception of the nature of technology among science teachers in the 1960s, and even later, was that technology was little more than the application of scientific knowledge and practices. The Organiser for Physics in the Nuffield Foundation's Science Teaching Project was doing no more than express a widely held belief when he stated that:

> The technologist must have a tremendous knowledge of science; and he must understand that science which he puts to such grand use . . . Furthermore I fear the technologist is sterile: one generation of technologists cannot breed the next generation – for the latter will be far behind the frontiers, and will lack the deeper understanding which is part of their preparation. It is the pure scientists who must give the next generation of technologists essential training.
>
> (Rogers, 1964)

Despite this attribution of low status to technology, many science teachers in the post-Nuffield period found it advantageous to incorporate references to technological applications in their work. The pure and academically demanding 'science for scientists' of the early projects was shown to have practical use outside the classroom as 'science for action'. Although this development helped to make the subject more attractive to students by relating science to the everyday and industrial worlds, the prime aim remained an understanding of scientific principles and not the development of a capability to identify and undertake successfully technological tasks. Technological applications were an addition designed to aid the learning of science.

A subsequent broadening of science courses involved consideration of social issues related to scientific developments and of the interactions between science, technology and society. The so-called STS movement achieved considerable prominence in the 1980s, although through most of this period there was little recognition by its practitioners of technology as anything other than an adjunct of science. The work of students might focus on a major technological advance such as nuclear power or human organ replacement, or on a current issue such as environmental pollution, the relevant science being studied alongside the societal aspects of it.

Recent STS teaching materials have recognised technology as an autonomous co-equal to, and not a subordinate branch of, science, but this was not so in the earlier 'science for citizens' developments. A position strongly argued by some science educators was that the introduction of technology as a separate field of study should be opposed; it would lead to science education becoming more pure because the applications of science would be dealt with in technology. Rather, technology should be 'incorporated into the context of science teaching' to enhance this; the content of present science courses should be taught 'in a technological way – applying, showing applications and teaching appreciation' of social and moral implications (Woolnough, 1975). Technology, then, was to remain subservient to science, assimilated into science education for the benefit of the latter, with the main road to pupils' technological understanding and capability being through science.

As we have seen, a direct challenge to this situation came in the 1980s with the development of CDT courses. An HMI survey, published in 1982, concluded that although 'in some areas the technology in CDT predominates . . . this is the exception rather than the norm'. At that stage, the development of technology courses was being undertaken by 'a small cadre of teachers, largely self-trained, male, constituting an evangelical vanguard amongst CDT teachers as a whole' (DES, 1982). Even so, the report was in no doubt that a course in technology had a strong claim on a place in the curriculum of all pupils until the statutory school leaving age. By the end of the decade, the Association for Science Education, in contrast to many of its previous statements about technology, was proclaiming a similar belief, that 'technological education should form an integral part of every pupil's liberal education' (ASE, 1988). Furthermore, a working party of Association members had been established to explore the contributions of science to technological education, not least when technology was taught as a separate subject in the secondary school curriculum. From a situation in which technology was a subordinate of science education, the reversal to science as a service subject for technology education had occurred with remarkable speed. Autonomous school technology had emerged on the curriculum landscape and the cuckoo in the nest of science education, now fully fledged, was requiring its foster parent to rethink its role.

Design and technology: The broad approach

With the implementation of the National Curriculum in England and Wales, the development of school technology moved a significant step forward. A Working Group on Design and Technology was established to advise on the attainment targets and programmes of study, its terms of reference being 'to view technology as that area of the curriculum in which pupils design and make useful objects or systems, thus developing their ability to solve practical problems'. Furthermore, the group was to assume 'that pupils will draw on knowledge and skills from a range of subject areas, but always involving science or mathematics'. Special reference was made to the contributions of art, business studies, CDT, home economics and information technology.

The view of technology which was eventually incorporated in the Statutory Order expressing the requirements for the subject was uniquely broad compared with its precursors. This breadth resided in several dimensions. First, the products of design and technology were described in the Order as 'artefacts, systems and environments'. Of course these are not clear-cut and mutually exclusive categories; a motor car is simultaneously an artefact, a collection of systems and an environment. The description was meant to signal to teachers that many activities which they had not previously thought of as 'design and technology' could, perhaps with some modification, be so regarded. It encouraged the recognition that designing and making a stage set for a production of *Romeo and Juliet*, the planning, preparation and delivery of inexpensive, nourishing meals to an old persons' home, and the design, construction and arrangements for maintenance of an environment for a hamster in a primary school classroom were all as valid design and technology activities as the making of a robotic arm to perform a manufacturing function.

A second dimension of breadth was provided by the designated contexts in which pupils were required to have experience of working. These were stated in the Order to be 'home, school, recreation, community, business and industry'. Not only did this range of contexts provide rich opportunities for pupils to identify tasks which would engage their motivation and commitment, but also a balanced experience of the use of different resources of knowledge and skills, and of operating within different constraints, was ensured.

The four attainment targets for design and technology (Table 2.1) provide further indications of the broad view of the subject which was

Table 2.1 National Curriculum attainment targets for design and technology from the 1990 Order

AT1	Pupils should be able to identify and state clearly needs and opportunities for design and technological activities through investigation of the contexts of home, school, recreation, community, business and industry
AT2	Pupils should be able to generate a design specification, explore ideas to produce a design proposal and develop it into a realistic, appropriate and achievable design
AT3	Pupils should be able to make artefacts, systems and environments, preparing and working to a plan and identifying, managing and using appropriate resources, including knowledge and processes
AT4	Pupils should be able to develop, communicate and act upon an evaluation of the processes, products and effects of their design and technological activities and of those of others, including those from other times and cultures

adopted. Attainment target 1 (AT1), for example, involved pupils in the unfamiliar and demanding task of problem construction. Needs and opportunities for design and technology activity do not exist, fully formed, in the various contexts that pupils investigate. Rather, they 'emerge' from the exercise of imagination, from the interplay of existing knowledge and expectations with new observations, and from the use of communication skills. The ability to identify and state a need or opportunity for design and technology activity is also related to the pupil's experience of visualising a design and technology response.

In working to achieve each of the attainment targets, pupils are inescapably faced with value judgements of many kinds and the emphasis on these exemplifies again the broad view of design and technology which has been adopted. Judgements about what is worthwhile and feasible initiate the activity. Judgements about the appropriateness of a design, and the means of realising it, shape the activity; and judgements about the functionality and effects of the product determine which steps are next required. The range of values involved is extensive, including technical, economic, aesthetic, social, environmental and moral, and design and technology activity is unavoidably concerned with the identification and reconciliation of conflicting values. There is never any single 'right answer' to a design and technology problem. What we encounter today in the made-world around us is the product of value judgements in the past, 'hardened history' as it has been called. An important aspect of technological capability is the recognition that there is nothing inevitable about technological development – it could all have been different, as an understanding of how other cultures have solved common technological problems constantly reminds us. Similarly, an essential element of an education in design and technology is a knowledge of the value options and decisions which have empowered the technological process in the past and which are doing so today. Attainment target 4, with its reference to an evaluation of the processes of design and technology in other times and cultures, has particular relevance to this point.

Last, but by no means least – if only because they relate directly to the subject of this book – the skills and knowledge necessary for design and technological capability contribute to the comprehensive view enshrined in the Order. The range of skills is much more extensive than those technical ones essential for executing tasks with materials, energy and information. Investigational, organisational and planning skills are needed. Similarly, communication in its broadest sense, involving not only talking, listening, reading, writing and graphical representation, but also the ability to persuade, negotiate, explain, criticise and accept criticism, is of paramount importance.

As for knowledge, it has been said that the corpus of knowledge upon which designers and technologists might need to draw is unbounded. It is not possible to prescribe a mandatory body of science or mathematics, for example, which is a necessary prerequisite for design and technology activity. Depending on the nature of the task and the imagination of the designer, different branches of craft, science and mathematics, as well as other subjects such as history, and different kinds of tacit 'know-how', might all be drawn upon.

Glen Aikenhead (1989) has used the example of designing and making a breathalyser to illustrate the disparate bodies of knowledge which can be called into play. In this case, they include a working knowledge of the body's respiratory and digestive systems, chemical changes, Henry's Law governing the pressure dependence of the solubility of gases in liquids and – according to the design route chosen – perhaps something on photometry or photoelectricity as well. Additionally, knowledge of the types of situation in which the breathalyser would be used and of consequent requirements (e.g. ergonomic and psychological considerations, police practice) would be necessary. The instrument's needed speed of response, health and safety regulations, potential market size, and mode and cost of manufacture could all be relevant items of information. If there were already in existence instruments to perform the same or similar tasks, their design and technology would need evaluation. The list could be extended.

Although at present few students in schools are likely to embark on tasks as demanding as the design and making of a breathalyser, the example illustrates the general point about the breadth of knowledge which may be necessary for successful design and technology activities. It also underscores what is the central concern of this book, the importance of science to the development of design and technology capability and, at the same time, the implications for science teachers of their subject having to take on the additional role of a resource for design and technology. Teaching about 'science *and* applications' or 'science *of* applications' is not the same as teaching 'science *for* applications'.

References

Aikenhead, G. (1989) *Logical Reasoning in Science and Technology*. Rexdale, Ontario: John Wiley.

Association for Science Education (1988) *Technological Education and Science in Schools*. Hatfield: ASE.

Department of Education and Science (1980) *Craft, Design and Technology in Schools: Some Successful Examples*. London: HMSO.

Department of Education and Science (1982) *Technology in Schools: Developments in Craft, Design and Technology Departments*. London: HMSO.

Department of Education and Science (1985) *The Curriculum from 5 to 16*. London: HMSO.

Joseph, K. (1985) Speech at Wembley Exhibition, 22 October 1985. DES Press Release.

McCulloch, G., Jenkins, E. and Layton, D. (1985) *Technological Revolution? The Politics of School Science and Technology in England and Wales since 1945*. London: Falmer Press.

Penfold, J. (1988) *Craft, Design and Technology: Past, Present and Future*. Stoke-on-Trent: Trentham Books.

Rogers, E. M. (1964) Teaching science for understanding. In Commonwealth Education Liaison Committee, *School Science Teaching*, pp. 18–27. London: HMSO.

Rose, M. (1988) Craft, design and technology. In K. Selkirk (ed.), *Assessment at 16*, pp. 166–85. London: Routledge.

Woolnough, B. E. (1975) The place of technology in schools. *School Science Review*, 156 (196), 443–8.

CHAPTER 3

Understanding technology – 1 The seamless web

Technology as an object of study

Although men and women have been engaged in the practice of technology since the beginning of history, our understanding of the nature of technology is very recent. In this connection, it is interesting to look briefly at the formal institutional structures that have been created to explore the nature of technology. By the opening of the second half of the twentieth century, there were sufficient scholars working in the field to support the foundation of a Society for the History of Technology (1958). The Society's journal, *Technology and Culture*, still pre-eminent in this area of research, has been published since 1959. A pioneering *Bibliography of the Philosophy of Technology* appeared first as a special number of *Technology and Culture* in 1973 and volume one of *Research in Philosophy and Technology*, the official publication of the Society for Philosophy and Technology, was published in 1978. Alongside these developments, and subsequently, university chairs and departments for the study of technology have been established. Regular international conferences are held for those working in the field, their activities now extending beyond history and philosophy into the sociology of technology.

It would be wrong to suggest that no interest had been shown in the practice, products and social interactions of technology prior to these developments. The chronicling of inventions, with a particular focus on their internal workings, goes back at least to the fifteenth century. In the nineteenth century, Samuel Smiles and others had written about the lives of great engineers, whilst in the early twentieth century A. P. Usher, Sigfried Giedion and Lewis Mumford had each published classic works on a central concern of their age, the mechanisation of the Western World. But it was not until the second half of the century that more general and institutionalised concerns for understanding technology became well-founded in academic societies, journals, conferences, university appointments and research.

It is interesting to set alongside this the rise of institutionalised concerns for the nature of science. These were predominantly products of the *first* half of the twentieth century. *Isis*, the leading journal for the history of science, commenced publication in 1912. The first British university department for the history and philosophy of science, at University College London, was founded in 1923. Karl Popper's seminal *Logik der Forschung* was published in Vienna in 1934 and several journals such as *Annals of Science, Ambix* and *Notes and Records of the Royal Society* date from the mid-1930s also. Without detailing events further, it would be true to say that the academic foundations for the original (but later reconstituted) Science Attainment Target 17 (the nature of science) in the National Curriculum of England and Wales were laid in the first five or six decades of this century.

Technology is not applied science

A question now arises as to why our understanding of technology has lagged behind that of science and has only recently become the focus of concerted academic exploration. One component of an answer to this is to be found in the first chapter where reasons for giving higher status to practical capability and for the recent incorporation of technology as a component of general education were reviewed. Economic success has become associated more with technology than with pure science. It is argued that despite producing more Nobel Prize winners in physics and chemistry per thousand of population than any other country, Britain's economy is still not competing effectively. We seem inept at converting scientific achievements into marketable and value-added products.

The previous assumption that technology is merely the application of science does not seem to bear fruit, and few today who have studied the relationship of science, technology and economic performance would subscribe to Lewis Mumford's assertion that:

> It was Henry who in essentials invented the telephone, not Morse; it was Faraday who invented the dynamo, not Siemens; it was Oersted who invented the electric motor, not Jacobi; it was Clerk Maxwell and Hertz who invented the radio telegraph, not Marconi and De Forest. The translation of the scientific knowledge into practical instruments was a mere incident in the process of invention.
>
> (Mumford, 1946: 217–18)

In contrast to this view, the historian of technology, Hugh Aitken, author of a classic study of the origins of radio, concludes that:

> . . . the content of the technological system that emerged from the work of Hertz, Lodge and Marconi was by no means uniquely determined by the nature of the scientific advances made by Faraday and Maxwell.
>
> (Aitken, 1985: 303)

and

> . . . while science played an essential role in making radiotelegraphy possible, it contributed little to the technology thereafter . . . A standard manual of the first decade of the twentieth century, such as Fleming's authoritative *Principles of Electric Wave Telegraphy* . . . is replete with detail on the design of apparatus and circuits but has nothing to say of scientific contributions once the basic phenomena of radiation and resonance are described. . . Even Fleming's diode valve, the strategic invention that ushered in the second phase in the history of radiocommunications, required no new scientific knowledge for its discovery. . . The same generalization can be made with reference to De Forest's triode vacuum tube, a device of major technological importance whose principles of operation the inventor himself did not understand and which certainly called for no new inputs of information from science.
>
> (Aitken, 1985: 326)

The image of abstract science as the engine impelling technological innovations was well burnished in the late nineteenth century and subsequently, not least by scientists. The discovery by the 19-year old William Henry Perkin of a synthetic dye, later marketed as Tyrian purple, was only one of a number of plausible and much quoted exemplars. To describe Perkin's work, as a President of the Chemical Society did in 1857, as 'a successful application of abstract science to an important practical purpose' was misleading, however. Not only had the discovery been accidental, but the process of application had been anything but routine and unproblematical. The task of scaling up from a laboratory bench experiment to the first multi-step, hazard-contained, industrial synthesis, yielding a product of quality and price acceptable to a substantial market, confronted Perkin with formidable problems, not only scientific and technological, but economic, environmental and legal also (Travis, 1990).

There is now general recognition that technology is more than 'the mere application of prior scientific knowledge', not least by economists. A distinguished member of that community, Nathan Rosenberg, has argued that 'technology is itself a body of knowledge about certain classes of events and activities'. He continues:

> It is a knowledge of techniques, methods, and designs that work, and that work in certain ways and with certain consequences, even when one cannot explain exactly why. It is . . . a form of knowledge which has generated a certain rate of economic progress for thousands of years. Indeed, if the human race had been confined to technologies that were understood in a scientific sense, it would have passed from the scene long ago.
>
> (Rosenberg, 1982: 143)

The development costs of modern aircraft are so enormous precisely because we have 'no theories of turbulence or compressibility adequate to determine optimal configurations in advance. Extensive testing and modification based upon test results are still required' (Rosenberg, 1982: 143). The situation is caricatured in the epigram: 'the engineer doesn't know why his bridge stays up: the scientist knows why his falls down'.

Who lays the golden eggs? Science or technology?

Another strand in the quest for improved national economic performance concerns the struggle for resources for scientific research. The view taken of the relationship between science and technology has sharp, practical consequences when applied to decisions about research funding. Should basic, curiosity-oriented research be the major beneficiary because it is supposed to yield, though unpredictably, the knowledge and stimulus for future material benefits? Or is the desired and unending succession of golden eggs more surely delivered by investment in mission-oriented research and development? Given the escalating costs of scientific research, questions about the most effective means of creating wealth from knowledge are inevitable.

After the Second World War, and capitalising on their contributions to impressive technological achievements which had helped to ensure victory, scientists in both the USA and Britain urged a concentration of research funds on basic science. In the USA, Vannevar Bush, science adviser to the president, argued that 'new products and new processes . . . are founded on new principles and new conceptions which in turn are painstakingly developed by research in the purest realms of science' (Bush, 1945: 13–14). Sometime later, in Britain, P.M.S. Blackett, as President of the Royal Society, submitted a memorandum to the Parliamentary Select Committee on Science and Technology on the most effective future allocation of research funds. His argument was premised on a model of innovation flowing from pure science: 'pure science, applied science, invention, development, prototype construction, production, marketing, sales and profits' (Blackett, 1968: 1108).

Subsequent attempts to quantify and prove these claims proved difficult and often inconclusive. In the USA, the Defense Department's Project Hindsight analysed 20 weapons systems adopted by the armed forces since the end of the war. Each system was broken down into innovative events in development. Out of a final total of 700 such events, only two appeared to be derived from basic scientific research. Ninety per cent of the remainder were classified as technological. This result was 'bad news' for the scientific community and was promptly challenged by a study at the Illinois Institute for Technology funded by the National Science Foundation (NSF), a not uninterested party. Called TRACES (an acronym for Technology in Retrospect and Critical Events in Science), this explored the genealogies of five 'high-technology' innovations, including the contraceptive pill, the electron microscope and videotape recording. In contrast to the Hindsight study, the NSF TRACES report claimed that 70 per cent of all the critical events in the development of these artefacts came from basic science.

Subsequent work in Britain and elsewhere has confirmed that science has in the past sometimes been 'over-sold' as the fount of material progress. However, it has also demonstrated that science is far from irrelevant, although its role is often a supporting rather than an initiating one. For example, it offers techniques and advice which can be critically important in the successful development of a technological innovation. The case of new tungsten–halogen lamp systems for cars illustrates the point.

> The problem was to introduce phosphorous and halogen into the lamp, and phosphonitrilic halides seemed to be a suitable form in which to introduce them. In initial tests, however, the lamps soon went black. Chemists at a nearby university suggested that the blacking was not due to decomposition of the phosphonitrilic halide itself but caused by impurities in the sample. Furthermore, they were able to provide a sensitive analytic technique for detecting the impurities. With pure samples, development of the innovation could proceed rapidly.
> (Jevons, 1976: 13–14)

The topic of science as a resource for the development of technological capability is the subject of a later chapter and is no more than broached here. It is clear, however, that simplistic models of the relationship between technology and science must be rejected. Alexander Keller (1984) has pointed out how, in an effort to capture something of the complexity and subtlety of the ways in which they have found science and technology to interact, researchers in this field have had to resort to metaphors. A few of these are illustrated below:

> Science is not the mother of invention but nursemaid to it: that is, she helps innovation to grow up. Moreover, she depends for her livelihood on making herself felt to be useful in this way. But she does not beget innovation, except very occasionally, illegitimately, under the backstairs so to speak.
> (Jevons, 1976: 18)

> Science acts as a background environment for technology; it is a pool in which industrialists can fish 'with greater or less success depending on their experience and expertise, and luck'. Because scientists are swimming in the pool they 'can draw the attention of fishermen to the location of the fish, or even present them with suitable specimens'.
> (Gibbons and Johnston, 1974: 241)

> Science and technology are 'mirror-image twins', two 'different communities, each with its own goals and systems of values'. The communities are interacting; some individuals straddle both; but the goals are different. 'The divisions between science and technology . . . are societal: they are between communities that value knowing and doing respectively'.
> (Layton, 1971: 565 and 1977: 209)

From technology as artefact to technology as system

Many of those who have studied the nature of technology have not done so from the standpoint of economics and with a prime focus on the role of technology in the creation of wealth. Criticism of the hierarchical dependence model of the science–technology relationships has come from several other directions. Historians, philosophers and sociologists have all contributed from their particular perspectives to enhance our understanding of the nature of technology.

Early excursions into the history of technology described the invention of artefacts in a chronological narrative. The workings of specific devices, the modifications and improvements made, and the range of applications provided the grist for the historian's mill. However, such internalist history offered little in the way of explanation why novel artefacts came into being and why they took the form they did. Attempts to provide answers to questions such as these obliged historians to explore the social, economic, political, legal and scientific contexts of invention, if not the psychology of inventors. In so doing, some historians such as Thomas Hughes, author of a prize-winning study of the introduction of electric light and power systems in Western society (Hughes, 1983), were led to view technology as part of a seamless web of interactive components in a complex socio-technical system. As Hughes notes, many of the technologists he studied 'were no respecters of knowledge categories or professional boundaries. In his notebooks, Thomas Edison so thoroughly mixed matters commonly labelled "economic", "technical" and "scientific" that his thoughts composed a seamless web' (Hughes, 1986: 285).

A related point about the nature of technology is made by Arnold Pacey in his excellent book *The*

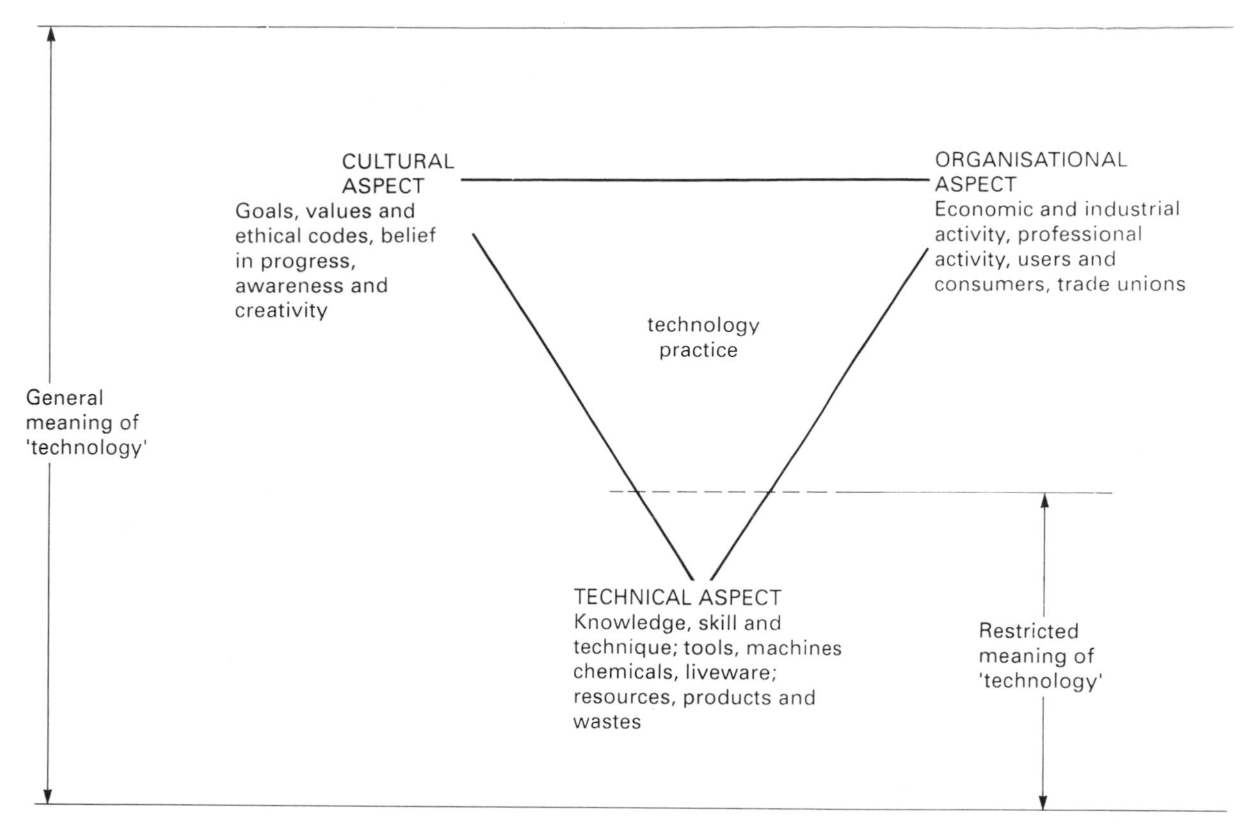

Fig. 3.1 Diagrammatic definition of 'technology' and 'technology practice' (from Pacey, 1983: 6).

Culture of Technology (1983). He draws an analogy with medicine, arguing that medical practice has not only a technical, but also an ethical and an organisational element to it, and that the same is true of technology practice. His diagrammatic representation of this (Fig. 3.1) is interpreted as follows. We tend to think first of the artefact (the motor car, the word processor, the infrared sensor in a domestic security system, the supermarket trolley, the greenhouse temperature control device) and the technical considerations (tools, skills) associated with it. This is a restricted meaning of technology. There is also, inevitably, what Pacey calls an organisational aspect and a cultural aspect to technology practice. The former involves, among other things, all those planning and organisational considerations associated with the production and use of the artefact. The latter is concerned with the values, beliefs and creative activity with which the artefact is imbued.

Stephen Kline, a mechanical engineer and professor of values, technology and society at Stanford University, comes to similar conclusions from an examination of the usages of the word 'technology'. He identifies four (Kline, 1985):

1 *Hardware (or artefacts)*: non-natural objects, of all kinds, manufactured by humans.
2 *Socio-technical system of manufacture*: all of the elements needed to manufacture a particular kind of hardware; the complete working system including its inputs – people, machinery,

resources, processes – and the legal, economic, political and physical environment.

3 *Technique, know-how or methodology*: the information, skills, processes and procedures for accomplishing tasks.

4 *Socio-technic system of use*: a system using combinations of hardware, people (and usually other elements) to accomplish tasks that humans cannot perform unaided by such systems – to extend human capacities.

The emphasis on values and value judgements is not as explicit in Kline's formulation as it is in Pacey's, but values are central to the construction of the two socio-technical systems Kline describes, and it is not difficult to map the two sets of categories on to each other.

Present-day experience of development projects in the Third World reinforces the need to adopt a view of technology which goes well beyond technical and scientific considerations to incorporate factors as diverse as: user values; financial, production and maintenance constraints; environmental impacts and political will. A well-documented case is UNICEF's rural water supply and sanitation programme in India.

A supply of potable water to rural villages is a major contribution to the health and well-being of those who live there. UNICEF's project in India began by the identification and drilling of reliable village boreholes which were then fitted with handpumps to deliver the water. Even with effective drilling techniques and efficient pumps, these installations were only as health-promoting as the sanitary practices of the users, so that an educational programme of basic hygiene was an essential accompaniment.

By 1974, of the handpumps fitted in over 9000 villages, some 75 per cent were out of action. No system for the supply of spare parts to village handymen was available and there was no maintenance training. It appeared that an investment of six million dollars had yielded little more than 9000 holes in the ground.

The problem was that the pumps that were installed were mostly cast-iron copies of farmstead pumps used in the USA and Europe. Whilst these were adequate for use by a single household, they were not designed to withstand continual daily use by an entire village community. The breakdown rate was high and repair difficult. As a result, attempts were made by various organisations to design a more reliable pump, appropriate to the particular demands of village use. Eventually, a pump was produced which met the stringent design criteria, including: low cost; durability; easy installation, maintenance and repair; and capable of being mass-produced under Indian conditions. A training programme in installation and maintenance procedures was initiated, and an instructional manual published.

A point of political significance was that the choice of an appropriate technology for the task, in this case a low-cost, 'simple' technology, had at times to overcome disdain from those at various levels in the administrative hierarchy, from government downwards. Not only politicians, but the technical bureaucracy in academia and industry, as well as users, had to be persuaded that the approach was sound and did not entail acceptance of a 'second-best' or professionally demeaning solution. Of course, when applied to technology, 'appropriate' does not necessarily mean 'primitive'. Techniques for discovering groundwater and for drilling through different kinds of geological formations need to be based on the best existing practice to achieve efficient solutions matched to the resources available. Furthermore, failure at some stage or other being a characteristic of all technological devices, even the best designed handpumps will break down. The design of pumps for ease of repair by those with little mechanical expertise represents a major challenge.

The location of individual pump units in separate villages entailed management of the system on a decentralised basis and, consequently, a high degree of user responsibility to keep the pump in good working order and to monitor the quality of water being delivered. Because women have had a traditional role in the use of water and waste disposal, it proved important to ensure that they were well represented in the development of infrastructures to support the system. It was the experience of the UNICEF project that most rural water and sanitation projects found it more difficult to create and set up mechanisms for keeping the system running effectively than to install it in the first instance. Establishing warehouses, effective lines of communication and procedures for the distribution of supplies were all part of the process of building capacity to implement and maintain the programme.

A further decentralising step involved the transfer of the technology to local manufacturers and suppliers. The intention here was to reduce the dependency of users on imported and centrally provided equipment. At the same time, it opened the door to a market in low-quality products, cheaper pumps, pipes and spare parts from 'pirate manufacturers'. It was necessary, therefore, to put in place a system of quality control involving the standardisation of parts, a list of approved manufacturers and training of local personnel in some operational and maintenance responsibilities. Such measures, particularly the last, could provoke opposition and resistance from those in established technical or managerial posts who feared their jobs and often meagre incomes were being threatened.

The achievement of community participation and readiness to practise self-help raised many problems. Siting a pump in a village brought into play considerations such as control of access by landowners, the relationship between proximity to the supply and responsibility for repairs, the needs of women who, although the main users, were rarely property owners, and the means by which caretaking and maintenance were to be provided. A complementary and often improvised health education programme had also to be established. In India, the small number of women who were handpump caretakers were the only health education agents linked directly to the UNICEF project. In Bangladesh, the handpump mechanics took on the role.

The ultimate goal of the Rural Water and Sanitation programme was to achieve a self-sustaining, consumer-driven service with characteristics including:

> . . . the majority of water supply repairs, some proportion of water supply installation (depending on technical feasibility) and almost all sanitation installation, is undertaken independently of the service authorities; the fuelling of demand by marketing and health education campaigns and the growth of public appreciation of service benefits; a change in the authorities' role to mainly supportive and backstopping instead of operational functions.
>
> (Black, 1990: 125)

At the time of writing her fascinating account of the UNICEF programme, from which the above example is drawn, Maggie Black was not able to report that this final stage had been reached in any of the various projects, in Bangladesh and Nigeria as well as in India. Nevertheless, she provides a rich picture of the seamless web in which a technological artefact, the village pump, is enmeshed. Only by the well-synchronised functioning of all components of the system is the technology likely to be successful. Also, as she notes, in terms of implementing the technological innovation, the hardware aspects (Pacey's restricted 'technical aspects' of technology practice) of drilling boreholes and constructing pumps represent a minor component only of the total challenge.

References

Aitken, H. G. J. (1985) *Syntony and Spark: The Origins of Radio*. Princeton, N.J.: Princeton University Press.

Black, M. (1990) *From Hand Pumps to Health: The Evolution of Water and Sanitation Programmes in Bangladesh, India and Nigeria*. New York: United Nations Children's Fund.

Blackett, P. M. S. (1968) Memorandum to the Select Committee on Science and Technology. *Nature*, 219, 1107–1110.

Bush, V. (1945) *Science, the Endless Frontier: A Report to the President*. Washington, D.C.: Office of Scientific Research and Development.

Gibbons, M. and Johnston, R. (1974) The roles of science in technological innovation. *Research Policy*, 3, 220–42.

Hughes, T. P. (1983) *Networks of Power: Electrification in Western Society*. Baltimore, MD.: Johns Hopkins University Press.

Hughes, T. P. (1986) The seamless web: technology,

science, etcetera, etcetera. *Social Studies of Science*, 16, 281–92.

Jevons, F. R. (1976) *Knowledge and Power*. Canberra: The Australian National University Advisory Committee on Science and Technology Policy Research.

Keller, A. (1984) Has science created technology? *Minerva*, 22, 160–82.

Kline, S. J. (1985) What is technology? *Bulletin of Science, Technology and Society*, 5(3), 215–18.

Layton, E. (1971) Mirror-image twins: The communities of science and technology in 19th century America. *Technology and Culture*, 12(4), 562–80.

Layton, E. (1977) Conditions of technological development. In I. Spiegel-Rosing and D. de Solla Price (eds), *Science, Technology and Society: A Cross-disciplinary Perspective*. London: Sage.

Mumford, L. (1946) *Technics and Civilization*. London: Routledge.

Pacey, A. (1983) *The Culture of Technology*. Oxford: Basil Blackwell.

Rosenberg, N. (1982) *Inside the Black Box: Technology and Economics*. Cambridge: Cambridge University Press.

Travis, A. S. (1990) Perkin's Mauve: ancestor of the organic chemical industry. *Technology and Culture*, 33, 51–82.

CHAPTER 4

Understanding technology – 2 Values, gender and reality

Technology and values

It has sometimes been argued that technology is 'neutral' or 'value-free'; it is the use made of the technology which determines whether it is 'good' or 'bad'. For example, it is said that an axe itself is 'neutral', but it can be used either constructively or destructively; similarly, a motor car can both save life (an ambulance) and destroy it ('joy-riding').

Whilst this argument might seem plausible, it does not stand up to close scrutiny. For one thing, as the case of the village handpumps has illustrated, it is difficult to isolate the material artefact from the network of human activities in which it is embedded and hence from the values of people. Also, an artefact, such as the motor car, can reshape people's values and call new ones into play. It makes possible new kinds of action between which people have to choose, i.e. they have to make value judgements. The availability of the chainsaw opened the way to rapid deforestation, with accompanying economic gain, but this was often achieved at the expense of ecological balance and the loss of rainforests. Because it created the new possibilities for action, can we call the chainsaw 'neutral'?

More obviously, the conception and realisation of a technological product entails some judgement about what is worthwhile as an outcome. In the view of the historian of technology, David Noble,

> . . . technology bears the social 'imprint' of its authors . . . there is always a range of possibilities or alternatives that are delimited over time – as some are selected and others denied – by the social choices of those with the power to choose, choices which reflect their intentions, ideology, social positions and relations with other people in society.
>
> (Noble, 1991: 14)

The simple cast-iron pump of European farmsteads was reflective of a certain style of social organisation; it did not transplant without major modification into a different cultural context from that of its origin.

Writing with the experience of technology transfer from industrialised to Third World countries in mind, Susantha Goonatilake goes further, describing technology as a social gene, a carrier of social relations from one society to another, which recreates in the recipient culture aspects of the social system of the donor:

> Technology . . . is a transmitter of social relations between social systems. In being adopted by its new host, it 'takes' elements from its new environment – hardware and knowledge as well as human operators – and rearranges them so that not only does it perform its technological function but also recreates aspects of the social system of its place of origin. It is thus like a virus, which enters a host cell whose component material it uses for its food as well as to reproduce itself.
>
> (Goonatilake, 1984: 122)

An example is the snowmobile in Lapland. Initially developed in North America and used for winter sports, the machine – rather like a motorcycle on skis – was introduced into Lapland and adopted for reindeer herding. The context of use here was quite different from that in North America, where prepared trails between tourist centres and service stations were available. The farmers in Lapland needed to acquire new skills to keep their snowmobiles working and to carry ample spares and fuel in case of breakdowns in situations remote from their base. Furthermore, the high capital and running costs of the machines meant that not every farmer was able to embark on the new mode of herding. Those who did were obliged by the economics of the technology to build up bigger herds of reindeer, buying out smaller farmers who then became waged labourers on the large farm units, or unemployed. Local industries supplying the needs of the old style of herding for sledges, skis and dogs went into decline and a dependence arose on foreign manufacturers of snowmobiles for spare parts. In summary, a predominantly egalitarian society where most owned and worked their own farms was transformed into an inegalitarian and hierarchical one. A new system of social relations had come into being.

A similar story can be told about the effects of the so-called green revolution in agricultural technology in Asia. American-inspired research had produced hybrid grain seeds which gave crops of outstanding yields. The transfer of these cereals to India, especially following the severe droughts of the mid-1960s, undoubtedly contributed to increased grain output. The use of the seeds, however, was only effective in conjunction with the application of chemical fertilisers and pesticides, and often required electric pump-driven irrigation systems. Also, new seeds had to be purchased each year. The capital-intensive nature of the green revolution made it of most benefit to those with large farms: the already prosperous grew more so, whilst the technology remained out of the reach of smaller and less well-off farmers. Goonatilake's (1984) conclusion is that the technology of the green revolution was far from being socially 'neutral': it was 'formed and governed by the social and economic conditions specific to the US of the time' (p. 136). For him, technology 'is history and social experience in concentrated form' (p. 139). This is similar to David Noble's conclusion derived from a detailed study of the development of industrial automation:

> Because of its very concreteness, people tend to confront technology as an irreducible brute fact, a given, a first cause, rather than as hardened history, frozen fragments of human and social endeavour.
>
> (Noble, 1984: xiii)

The technology does not have to be as it is. Other options have been available: what we encounter is the result of decisions which reflect the value judgements of those who shaped a development which was not inevitable.

Accepting that there is social determination of technology, it remains the case that simple observation of an artefact does not usually allow us to discern the inherent values. Values – technical, social, political, environmental, aesthetic or ethical – do not stand out on the surface of, say, a telephone handpiece or a hairdryer. However, when the technology is viewed from the perspective of transfer from the cultural context of origin to a different cultural context, then, as we have seen, values are uncovered. Similarly, when considered from the standpoint of adoption – why *this* technological artefact rather than *that* became widely used – values become visible. Writing about the introduction of steam power technology in Sweden in the early eighteenth century, the sociologist of technology, John Law, has stated that:

> . . . the success of technology is not a transparent issue that has to do with machinery alone, but also, and more basically has to do with judgements of adequacy by relevant social groups . . . Successful technologists are also social engineers – they operate not only upon networks of interrelated objects, but also, and simultaneously, upon sets of social and economic relations.
>
> (Law, 1987: 568)

In short, the values in the technology must match those of its users. When they do not, technology obsolescence, the inverse of adoption, occurs. Increased concerns for the quality of the environment and the rise to prominence of 'green values' have, for example, led to the replacement of some manufacturing processes by new ones which reduce emissions of sulphur dioxide and the so-called greenhouse gases.

Whilst the intimate connection between technology and value judgements is not in question and it is clear that social preferences do influence technological developments, it does not follow that technology is totally under human control. Indeed, the counter proposition, technological determinism, maintains that technology has become autonomous, a force which, Frankenstein-like, has now taken over. Far from being society's servant, technology is society's master, shaping our destinies in ways which seem inevitable and irreversible.

Even if we baulk at the prospect of extreme technological determinism, there is general agreement that the full extent of the social effects of technological innovations is difficult if not impossible to predict. Technology frequently seems to lead a double life: whilst it can fulfil the most exorbitant intentions of its practitioners, such as landing a man on the moon and creating weapons systems of unprecedented destruction, it also, and simultaneously, produces unintended outcomes. Medical technologies have reduced the death rate in developing countries, but have also contributed to uncontrollable population growth. Food production has become more efficient through genetic and chemical technologies, but at the cost of damage to related ecosystems. No one planned or wanted the effects which DDT has had on bird populations, for example, and no one intended to create a hole in the ozone layer. In an attempt to exercise greater control over the effects of technological developments, a new branch of study called Technology Assessment has come into being. An example of the scope of technology assessment as well as of the range of intended and unintended effects of one particular technology, the automobile, is shown in Table 4.1. Concern over the control of technology has been one of the strongest motivations for the increased efforts to understand technology which were described at the beginning of Chapter 3.

Gender and technology

Unlike sex, gender is not a biological or behavioural reality. It is a construct, shaped over the years in ways which have resulted in certain characteristics and domains of human experience being associated with men and others with women, and with the categories of 'masculine' and 'feminine', respectively.

This 'gendering' of experience is nowhere more obvious than in technology. We have come to link men with qualities such as assertiveness, aggression, rationality and materialism, along with high-profile technologies to do with machines, computers, control, construction, exploration and warfare. Likewise, women have come to be associated with nurturance, emotionality, passivity and piety; in so far as they have been seen to have involvements with technologies, these have been life-sustaining and life-enhancing (though often unsung), related to food, textiles, decoration, childrearing and domesticity. Indeed, the gender-riven nature of technology is even more profound than this. We have tended not to think of what women do as in any sense technological, despite their involvements in survival technologies since the dawn of history. As Patricia Hynes (1989: 9) has expressed it: 'Women have never lived without technology. Yet we have barely a toehold in the discourse and direction of it.'

The point is reinforced by the fact that most people would have difficulty in naming, say, six women technologists from the whole span of human history. No such problem would be encountered in the case of men. The great road makers, fen drainers, canal and bridge builders and lighthouse constructors were eulogised in nineteenth-century popular writings such as those of Samuel Smiles, and heroic accounts of their achievements were incorporated into the school books of the times. Smiles called one of his works *Men of Invention and Industry* (1884), and it is not uncommon in later histories of technology to find chapters and headings such as 'Men of steam' or 'The men who made the railways'. To quote Patricia Hynes (1989) again, women 'have been robbed of the history of female technical initiative,

Table 4.1 How the automobile has altered our lives (from *New Scientist*, 24 May 1973, p. 469)

Technology assessment must look as far beyond the immediate impact of new technology as possible. The following list of selected impacts of the automobile on society shows just how far reaching these impacts can be, and how wide a TA exercise must cast its net. Gabor Strasser, director of planning, Columbus Laboratories, Battelle Memorial Institute, Columbus, Ohio, includes this list in a contribution to the book *Technology Assessment in a Dynamic Environment* (Gordon & Breach).

Selected impacts of the automobile (1895 to present)

Values

Geographic mobility
Expansion of personal freedom
Prestige and material status derived from automobile ownership
Over-evaluation of automobile as an extension of the self – an identity machine
Privacy – insulates from both environment and human contact
Consideration of automobile ownership as an essential part of normal living (household goods)
Development of automobile cultists (group identification symbolised by type of automobile owned)

Environment

Noise pollution
Automobile junkyards
Roadside litter

Social

Changes in patterns of courtship, socialisation and training of children, work habits, use of leisure time, and family patterns
Created broad American middle class, and reduced class differences
Created new class of semi-skilled industrial workers
Substitution of automobile for mass transit
Ready conversion of the heavy industrial capability of automobile factories during World War II to make weapons
Many impacts on crime
Increased tourism
Changes in education through bussing (consolidated school versus 'one room country schoolhouse')
Medical care and other emergency services more rapidly available
Traffic congestion
Annual loss of life from automobile accidents about 60 000
Increased incidence of respiratory ailments, heart disease and cancer
Older, poorer neighbourhood displacement through urban freeway construction

Institutional

Automotive labour union activity set many precedents
Decentralised, multidivisional structure of the modern industrial corporation evident throughout the auto industry
Modern management techniques
Consumer instalment credit
Unparalleled standard of living
Emergence of US as foremost commercial and military power in world
Expansion of field of insurance
Rise of entrepreneurship
Basis for an oligopolistic model for other sectors of the economy
Land usage for highways – takes away from recreation, housing, etc
Land erosion from highway construction
Water pollution (oil in streams from road run-off)
Unsightly billboards
Air pollution – lead, asbestos, HC, CO, NO_x, SO_x

Demography

Population movement to suburbs
Shifts in geographic sites of principle US manufacturers
Displacement of agricultural workers from rural to urban areas
Movement of business and industry to suburbs
Increased geographic mobility

Economic

Mainstay and prime mover of American economy in the 20th century
Large number of jobs directly related to automobile industry (one out of every six)
Automobile industry the lifeblood of many other major industries
Rise of small businesses such as service stations and tourist accommodations
Suburban real estate boom
Drastic decline of horse, carriage and wagon businesses
Depletion of fuel reserves
Stimulus to exploration for drilling of new oil fields and development of new refining techniques, resulting in cheaper and more sophisticated methods
Increased expenditure for road expansion and improvement
Increased federal, state and local revenues through automobile and gasoline sales taxes
Decline of railroads (both passengers and freight)
Federal regulation of interstate highways and commerce as a pattern for other fields
Highway lobby – its powerful influence

imagination and invention. We have lost our place in defining and shaping technology' (p. 11). She continues:

> In most developing countries, women tend woodlots, do subsistence farming and are responsible for water supply and waste disposal. Yet development aid and technologies exogenously introduced into these countries have ignored women's knowledge and failed to engage them in the design and use of new technologies. They often destroy the environmental base which has traditionally been used and conserved by women. In the so-called developed world, laboratories, research institutes and companies are modelled on the patriarchal family, where women function as assistants to fathers, husbands, brothers or sons.

It is important to recognise this deep historic 'gendering' process if we are to begin to understand technology today. We have come to regard it as a masculine preserve and, conversely, to see it as neither feminine nor a place for women. Women's roles have been limited to those of users and consumers, with design, decision making and development monopolised by men. In the UK, over 80 per cent of computer users are women; in contrast, the proportion of females among computer science undergraduates is approximately 10 per cent. Jan Zimmerman's argument below might have been better expressed in terms of masculine-gender values rather than male-sex attributes, but the general point holds good, nevertheless:

> Our communication technologies are invented by men who don't like to talk to other people. Our offices are designed by men who prefer isolation. Our cities are laid out by men who crave distance from others. Our utilities are generated by men who prefer to depend on machines than on other human beings . . . we seek high-tech refuge from high-tech because the human being has been left out; the female part of all of us is missing and we miss it. If that doesn't explain why we need more female engineers, nothing will.
>
> (Zimmerman, 1986: 53)

Put differently, by adopting the perspective of gender, we are helped to transcend historic assumptions about masculine and feminine roles in technology and to appreciate how our perceptions and practice of technology have been distorted. More positively, a new, challenging and richer prospect of technology comes into focus.

We are led, for example, to adopt a more inclusive view of the scope of technological activities. Once we move beyond a view of technology as artefacts, and see it as a social phenomenon, an expression of human work, the question 'what counts as work?' becomes important. The traditional response to this has been in terms of the kinds of paid work undertaken by men. However, it is the case that women, who make up one-half of the global population and one-third of the labour force, are responsible for two-thirds of all working hours (Rothschild, 1989: 202). Much of this work is unpaid; the women receive only one-tenth of world income. Possibly because of its unrewarded nature, most of the work that women do has hitherto been judged to fall outside the ambit of technology. Revision of this judgement, in the light of gender considerations, brings into the sphere of technology a range of new activities associated with, for example, the home, the office, clothing, reproduction, nutrition, health and healing. Re-enfranchising this major segment of unpaid work by women within the bounds of technology will hopefully lead to a different representation of it in cultural life and encourage more democratic forms of control.

Recognition that the historic gender associations in technology are not immutable has led to the revision of several aspects of our assessment of the social, economic and political effects of technological innovations. For example, it has been widely assumed that household technology has liberated women from domestic servitude and opened the way to other employment in offices and factories. More recent evidence appears to show that this is not the case. Despite technological changes which have reduced the physical strength and skills needed for many jobs, women in industry are still concentrated in the less mechanised occupations, whilst on the domestic front 'the sex, hours, efficiency and status of the household worker' are largely unchanged (McGaw, 1989).

However, women have been far from passive receivers of household technology. They have used it to achieve ends which the designers and producers had not prioritised. In their hands, it became a means to longer, healthier lives, more regular school attendance, upward occupational mobility and, overall, a higher standard of living. In turn, this testified to the virtues of industrialisation to those who viewed it from outside. Only occasionally, the downside has been acknowledged, as when Gandhi, about to board his 'plane at the end of his first visit to the UK, was asked by a reporter, 'What do you think about Western civilization?' After a moment for reflection, the reply came, 'Yes, I think it would be a good idea'. There is a salutary reminder here that the criteria for judging what is technological progress are by no means universal.

'School technology' and 'real technology'

The picture of technology which this chapter and the previous one have tried to sketch is one of a complex, creative and constrained activity, drawing upon science as well as other knowledge resources, but nevertheless very different from science in many ways. It is also a picture of an activity infused with value considerations of diverse kinds and whose products, whilst carrying the imprint of their social origins, can in turn reshape society, often in unpredictable ways. A question now arises about the extent to which 'school technology' corresponds to this portrayal.

One strand of evidence which supplies a partial answer to this question is to be found in school textbooks and curriculum materials, and especially in the so-called 'models' of design and technology activity which appear there. Some of these are intended to represent the interactive nature of the processes involved, two of them being illustrated in Figs 4.1 and 4.2. These attempts to capture 'thought in action' are undoubtedly helpful for teaching and examining; indeed, it has been argued that the 'inter-relationship between modelling ideas in the mind, and modelling ideas in reality is the cornerstone of capability in design and technology' (Kimbell *et al.*, 1991: 21).

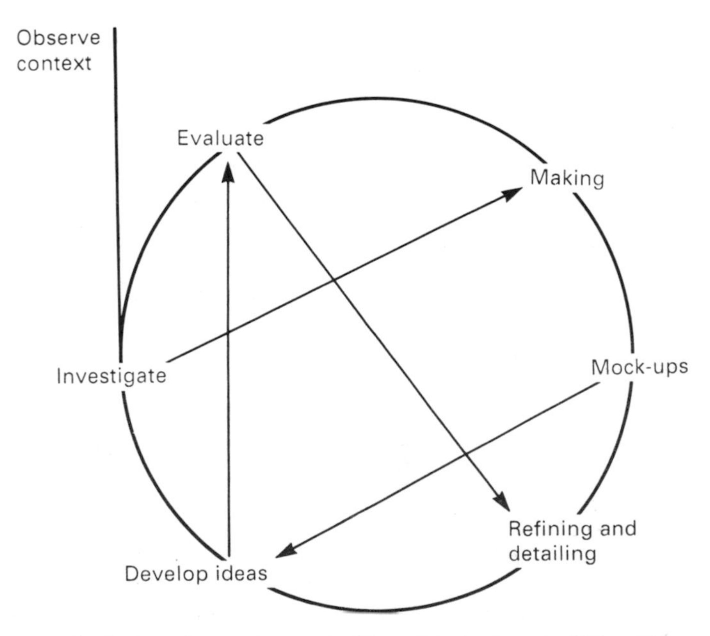

Fig. 4.1 A representation of the interactive design cycle (from Kimbell *et al.*, 1991: 19).

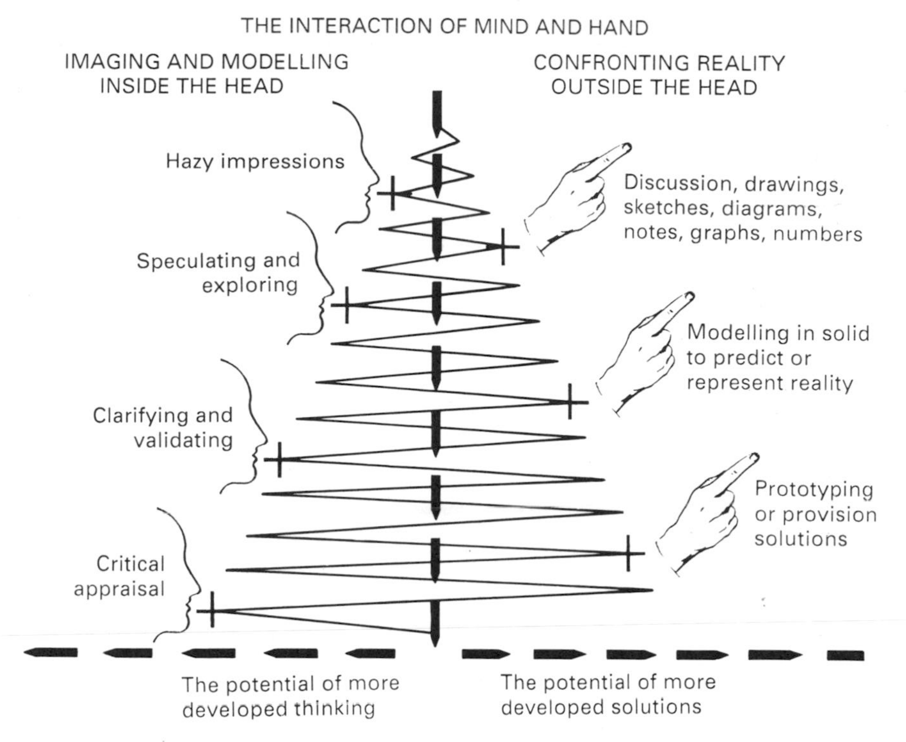

Fig. 4.2 The APU model of interaction between mind and hand (from Kimbell *et al.*, 1991: 20).

However, they fail to represent some essential aspects of design and technology, perhaps their most significant weakness being their silence on what might be called the politics of the activity, i.e. who shapes the decisions at various points in the process and in terms of what value considerations. They also imply an individualism which is rarely encountered in the 'real-world' technology where teamwork and collaboration are the norm.

It is not that such 'cognitive-processes' models of technology are 'wrong', but that, on their own, they tell only part of the story and need complementing by others such as the socio-political model of Pacey in Fig. 3.1. A different 'conceptual framework for technology' that attempts to capture significant features of 'real technology' to inform the development of school programmes is that of Marc de Vries in the Netherlands (Peters *et al.*, 1989: 239; see Fig. 4.3). He claims to have incorporated five characteristics of technology in his scheme:

1 Technology is a human activity, both for women and for men.
2 Technology uses matter, energy and information as input.
3 Technology and science are interrelated.
4 Technology is a process of designing, making and using products.
5 Technology and society are interrelated.

Whilst the 'model' leaves many questions unanswered, and the interactive nature of 'designing, making and using' appears to have been lost, the cast of actors in the drama is richer and the cultural embeddedness of technology is portrayed. The proposals which stem from the model for the content of technology education in Dutch secondary schools identify three 'subject components': technology and society; working with products of technology; and producing technology. This raises a question about the mutual independence of these three curriculum strands.

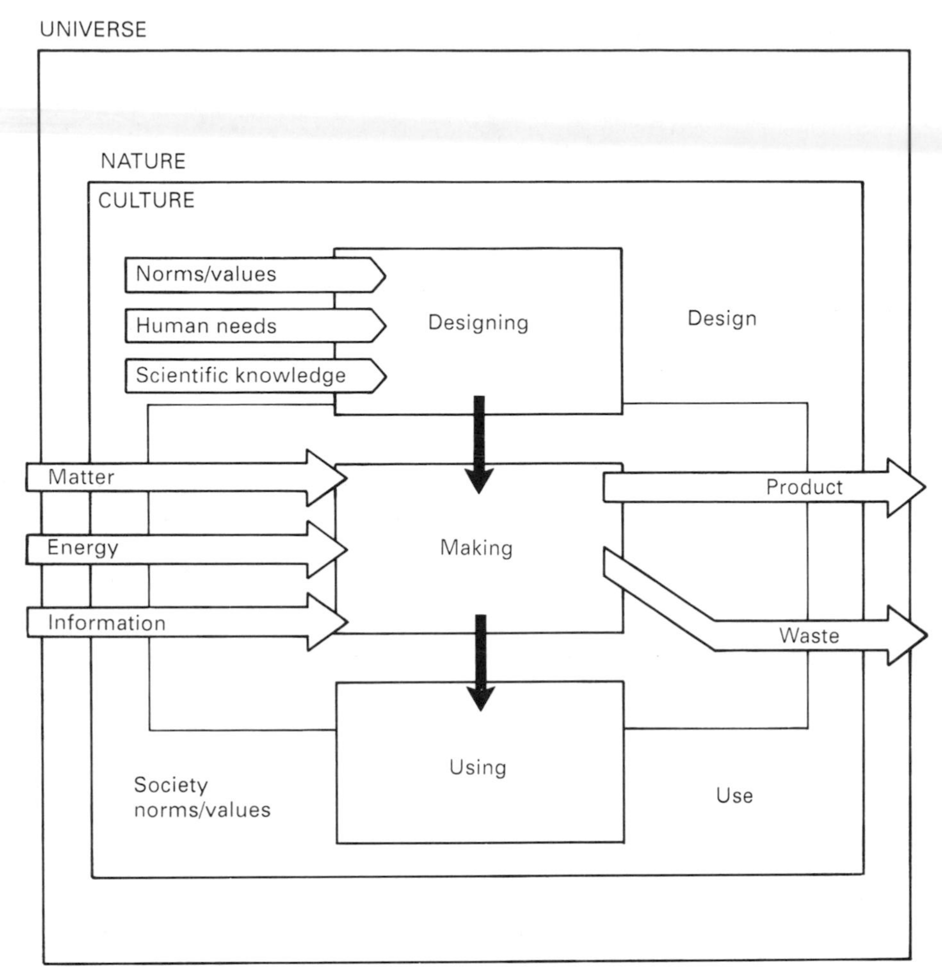

Fig. 4.3 Conceptual framework for technology developed at the Pedagogisch Technische Hogeschool, the Netherlands.

No such distinctions are found in the 1990 Statutory Order for Technology in the National Curriculum of England and Wales. Although not in diagrammatic form, as previous models have been, the Order does provide a representation of technology in the attainment targets, statements of attainment and programmes of study laid down. Here, knowledge of the interactions of technology and society and experience of working with technologies are resources inseparable from the acts of designing, making and evaluating and the development of design and technological capability. In relation to attainment target 1 (identifying needs and opportunities for design and technological activities), for example, in order to achieve attainment level 5, pupils must be able to 'recognise that economic, social, environmental and technological considerations are important'. In the case of attainment target 3 (planning and making), to achieve level 6, pupils must be able to 'use knowledge of materials, components, tools, equipment and processes, to change working procedures to overcome obstacles as making proceeds'. Perhaps the best example is attainment target 4, however, which requires pupils to 'act upon an evaluation of the processes, products and effects' of their own design and technological activities and 'of those of others, including those from other times and cultures'. To satisfy this requirement, they must, among other attainments:

- understand the social and economic effects of some artefacts, systems or environments [level 4];
- understand that artefacts, systems or environments from other times and cultures have identifiable characteristics and styles, and draw upon this knowledge in design and technological activities [level 5];
- evaluate the ways in which materials have been used [level 6];
- understand that artefacts, systems or environments reflect the circumstances and values of particular cultures and communities [level 8].

This emphasis on integration of knowledge of previous technological achievements and of the cultural variety of technological responses to problems, is reflective of much technology in the 'real world'. Technological traditions have been forged there around modes of training, skill development (often in master/apprentice relationships) and knowledge of previous successes and failures. Much of this technological activity has involved the incremental and progressive improvement of existing artefacts and devices. By analogy with Thomas Kuhn's distinction between 'normal' and 'revolutionary' science, such work might be described as 'normal technology'. The quest for gains in artefactual characteristics such as speed, power or efficiency has been undertaken within a constraining paradigm of decisions about operational principles and artefact configurations.

Aeroplane design provides a good illustration. The operational principle here derives from the fact that the flow of air over the top surface of a moving, curved aerofoil is faster than that over the lower surface. As a result, the pressure of air below the wing is greater than that above and this 'lifts' the wing. The familiar configuration to put this into effect is the tubular body with engine forward, tail aft and lateral wing planes. But it does not have to be so. Alternatives exist; both the operational principle and the configuration can be changed, as in the helicopter which flies without wings. In the case of vertical take-off and landing aircraft, the engine may be in the tail.

If incremental improvements or applications within a technological tradition, embodying continuity of practice in design and making, constitute 'normal technology', then artefactual discontinuity, the result of radical innovation in design conception and realisation, is what corresponds to Kuhn's 'revolutionary science'. The history of technology shows that increasingly, and especially in modern times, an important source of innovatory principles for revolutionary technology has been scientific knowledge. As noted earlier, however, its use is rarely a matter of simple application.

Not all that children do in 'school technology' can or need be 'revolutionary', although the use of a new operational principle with which to attack a technological problem in, for them, a novel way, may count as this. There is considerable educational profit, however, in the critical evaluation and progressive improvement of existing artefacts and systems, and the development of new ways of using them. The laser provides a 'real technology' example here: at the time of its discovery, no one could foresee among its many future applications its use in dermatology for the removal of 'port wine' birthmarks. Its adaptation for precision work in this field represents a distinct technological achievement. Whatever form 'school technology' takes, however – 'normal' or 'revolutionary' – it is important that the resources of science are accessible to and exploited by it. A 'school technology' which was not symbiotic with science would fall short of 'real technology' in disabling ways.

References

Goonatilake, S. (1984) *Aborted Discovery: Science and Creativity in the Third World*. London: Zed Books.

Hynes, H. P. (ed.) (1989) *Reconstructing Babylon: Women and Technology*. London: Earthscan Publications.

Kimbell, R., Stables, K., Wheeler, T., Wosniak, A. and Kelly, V. (1991) *The Assessment of Performance in Design and Technology*. London: School Examinations and Assessment Council.

Law, J. (1987) Review of S. Lindquist, technology on trial: the introduction of steam power into Sweden, 1715–1736. *Social Studies of Science*, 17(3), 564–9.

McGaw, J. (1989) No passive victims, no separate spheres: A feminist perspective on technology's history. In S. H. Cutcliffe and R. C. Post (eds), *In Context: History and the History of Technology*, pp. 172–91. London: Associated Universities Press.

Noble, D. (1984) *Forces of Production: A Social History of Industrial Automation*. New York: Alfred A. Knopf.

Noble, D. (1991) Social choice in machine design: The case of automatically controlled tools. In H. Mackey, M. Young and J. Beynon (eds), *Understanding Technology in Education*. London: Falmer Press.

Peters, H., Verhoeven, H. and de Vries, M. (1989) Teacher training for school technology at the Dutch Pedagogical Technological College. In M. J. de Vries (ed.), *Report PATT 4 Conference: Teacher Education for School Technology*. Eindhoven: PTH.

Rothschild, J. (1989) From sex to gender in the history of technology. In S. H. Cutcliffe and R. C. Post (eds), *In Context: History and the History of Technology*, pp. 192–203. London: Associated Universities Press.

Zimmerman, J. (1986) *Once upon a Future: A Woman's Guide to Tomorrow's Technology*. London: Pandora Press.

CHAPTER 5

Science as a resource for technological capability

Some preliminary issues of definition and scope

That science and technology are intimately connected is not in question. After all, science prescribes the so-called 'laws of nature' within which all technological activity is obliged to take place. For example, technological contrivances cannot flout the law of conservation of energy or the tendency for energy to always change from more useful to less useful forms. It is also clear that technology is much more than 'mere applied science'.

In exploring the relationship, a first step is perhaps the recognition that the terms 'science' and 'technology' do not stand for activities which are distinct and unrelated. Certainly, at the level of individual scientists and technologists today, whether in industry or academia, their work may entail both scientific investigations and experimentation *and* the design and construction of new systems and instrumentalities of various kinds. This is not to say that the activities are identical, but that they are inextricably linked in much day-to-day professional activity.

Furthermore, 'science' is not an unambiguous term; it frequently needs to be qualified to convey the different emphases it can be given. An example is found in the debate over funding of scientific research in Britain in the early 1970s (Senker, 1991). The central issue here was the extent to which it was possible to establish a distinction between pure and applied scientific research. Lord Rothschild, head of the government's Central Policy Review staff, argued, in opposition to the Council for Scientific Policy, that the consumer–contractor principle provided the means of doing this. His view was that, in the applied sphere,

> The customer says what he wants; the contractor does it (if he can); and the customer pays . . . Basic, fundamental or pure research . . . has no analogous customer–contractor basis.
>
> (Rothschild, 1971: 3)

Later experience suggested that there was often a pre-development gap between completion of academic research and the demonstration that it could yield a marketable product within a reasonable time. This led to the concept of 'strategic science' to denote research additional and parallel to basic research. Its aim was:

> . . . to achieve national strategic objectives that may originate from either of two directions (i) market pull, when a potential user has recognised that more background knowledge in a particular field is needed, and (ii) technology push, when research workers have recognised that a discovery may lead on to practical applications.
>
> (Mason, 1983)

Developing this idea, the Advisory Council for Applied Research and Development (ACARD) presented a report to Margaret Thatcher, the then

Prime Minister, on *Exploitable Areas of Science*, an exploitable area being defined as:

> . . . one in which the body of scientific understanding supports a generic (or enabling) area of technological knowledge; a body of knowledge out of which many specific products and processes may emerge in the future.
> (ACARD, 1986: 11)

Without going further, it appears that distinctions, though not precise boundaries, can be drawn between:

- *pure/fundamental science*: driven by curiosity and speculation about the natural world without thought of possible applications;
- *strategic science*: yielding a reservoir of knowledge, out of which the as yet unidentified winning products and processes will emerge; and
- *applied science*: related to a specific project and tied closely to a timetable with a practical outcome often specified by a 'customer'.

In other words, science is not a uniform activity and form of knowledge. There is a spectrum of possibilities and, as the ACARD report expressed it, 'science comes in an infinite variety of shapes and sizes' (1986: 15). The content of school science, however, has historically been drawn very largely from the first of the three categories above.

Technology, similarly, is diversified and plural. Generic or enabling technologies, sometimes called key technologies, have been highlighted in many recent discussions about the means by which industries can be made more competitive. These are technologies which have the potential to be applied widely across the industrial civil and military sectors. The list usually includes:

> - information and communications technology;
> - advanced industrial materials technology;
> - biotechnology; and
> - advanced manufacturing technology.
>
> (Further Education Unit, 1988: 8)

and converges with areas of strategic science. The full range of technologies is much wider, however. In addition to the above, the American Association for the Advancement of Science Project 2061 identified technologies of energy, agriculture and food, medicine, the environment, electronics, computers, transportation and space as being rich sources of themes and concepts for the technology education of high school students (Johnson, 1989). The list could be extended without difficulty, and comparison with the content of most previous school technology programmes serves to emphasise the narrow range of technologies upon which the latter have traditionally drawn.

In exploring the ways in which science can act as a resource for technological activities, it will be important to keep in mind that neither science nor technology is a single, uniform, unchanging entity. It will also help to recognise some distinctions between the ways in which science and technology have already been drawn into relationships in the school curriculum.

1 Science and/with *technology*

Although the reformed science programmes of the early 1960s were remarkably 'pure', subsequent curriculum developments have incorporated technological applications and illustrations of 'science in action' to a considerable degree. The reasons for this have been analysed elsewhere (e.g. Fensham 1991) and need not be detailed here. For present purposes, the significant point is that the courses have been structured in terms of scientific concepts and principles, with the technology being 'added on' to illustrate the application of the science in situations likely to enhance students' interest in, and understanding of, the science. Programmes with titles such as Science at Work and Physics Plus/Chemistry Plus/Biology Plus are representative of this genre.

2 Science of *technology*

Again with the prime aim of improving the learning of science, other courses were developed that began with a technological context or application from which scientific principles and concepts were then derived. Such applications-led or context-based approaches, often termed 'concepts-in-context' courses, are exemplified by Salters' Science and Salters' Chemistry in Britain and Chemistry in the Community (Chemcom) in the USA. Although the science and technology were drawn into a close relationship, the partnership was primarily designed to serve the ends of science education. Such learning about technology that occurred was, as in the previous case, incidental and secondary to the understanding of science.

3 Science **for** *technology*

Quite different from each of the two previous cases is that in which the development of students' technological capability is the main aim and the science is treated as a resource, along with other forms of knowledge and skills, in order to achieve this end. Such a relationship between science and technology entails a substantial role change for science: from a major discipline in its own right, studied for its own sake, it becomes a service subject. The cathedral is transformed into a quarry, or, as one philosopher of technology has expressed it, pure science becomes 'a servant to technology, a charwoman serving technological progress' (Skolimowski, 1966: 373).

4 Science–Technology–Society (STS) courses

Before exploring this role change in greater detail, one further science education development requires comment. Throughout the 1980s, Science–Technology–Society (STS) programmes were developed in many countries. Technology here was not necessarily subservient to science, although in fact few of the earlier courses acknowledged technology as more than 'applied science', inseparable from and dependent upon it. The focus was on societal issues and topics with a strong science and technology dimension and the main contribution to the aims of an autonomous technology education was through 'technological awareness', i.e. awareness of the personal, social, moral, economic and environmental implications of technological developments. Later attempts to provide a conceptual framework for STS courses have, however, given greater prominence to understanding the nature of technology and its interactions with science and society (Aikenhead, 1986; Bybee, 1987; Layton, 1988). This tends to be at a theoretical level, however, often based on case studies or simulations, and the opportunities for students on STS courses to engage practically in the design and construction of technological interventions in 'real-world' situations remains limited. Personal involvement in technological activities intended to develop design and technological capability, in its widest sense, has not been a distinguishing feature of STS programmes.

Science as a resource: Some specific examples

Because the ways in which science can contribute to the development of technological capability are many and often complex, it may be helpful to begin with some of the simpler and more obvious examples. These are cases in which scientific knowledge and technique are brought to bear upon aspects of a technological task directly and without need for any substantial modification of the science.

Systematic empirical enquiry

Questions such as 'Will this material serve for this purpose?' or 'Which of these materials is most suitable for this job?' often arise in design and technological activities. Sometimes the properties of the materials have already been studied and the answer to the questions can be found in scientific tables, e.g. the thermal conductivity of a solid material such as cork. Often, however, it will be necessary to design and conduct a small-scale investigation into the working properties of the materials in question, e.g. which of these available materials best repels water under these particular conditions? The ability to identify and control variables, to engage in quantitative modes of working, and to systematically experiment to optimise performance of a device are all skills which can be borrowed from science and brought to bear fruitfully on technological activities.

It was by these means that the Leeds engineer, John Smeaton, in the eighteenth century, achieved notable improvements to the efficiency of the Newcomen steam engine. According to a later writer, Smeaton's practice:

> . . . was to adjust the engine to good working order, and then after making a careful observation of its performance in that state, some one circumstance was altered, in quantity or proportion, and then the effect of the engine was tried under such change; all the circumstances except the one which was the object of the experiment, being kept as nearly as possible unchanged.
>
> (Cardwell, 1972: 83, citing John Farey's *A Treatise on the Steam Engine*, London, 1827)

The method of establishing facts by carefully controlled experiments is an important contribution of science to technology, whether it is at the level of industry (e.g. determining the optimum aerodynamic shape of a new car), of a secondary school project (e.g. devising a means of ascertaining whether an electric blanket is safe to use after a period of summer storage), or of primary school pupils thinking up a 'fair test' of possible constructional materials.

Quality assurance and control

A second way in which science serves technology is by contributing to the assurance and control of the quality of technological products and of the components and materials used in their production. The use of analytical techniques by chemists to identify and remove an impurity in phosphonitrilic halides was critical to the successful manufacture of tungsten–halogen lamps (see p. 26). Many similar examples of the use of chemical techniques could be given. The treatment of sewage and the provision of a safe supply of drinking water to city dwellers are obvious cases of technological processes where constant quality control is essential to the health of the community. The techniques of hazardous waste disposal, and of monitoring environmental quality generally, rely heavily on a knowledge of chemistry and use of chemical techniques.

The case of polychlorinated biphenyls (PCBs) is illustrative. Approximately one million tons of PCBs have been produced since manufacture started in 1929. These substances are very resistant to attack by acids, alkalis and (other than at very high temperatures) heat, and have been widely used in industry as cooling fluids in large transformers, as insulation in capacitors, in hydraulic systems, heat exchangers, paints, adhesives, printing inks, carbonless copying paper, lubricants and flameproof fabrics. A considerable part of this production has already been released into the environment as industrial and commercial waste; in addition, it is estimated that at least 250 000 tons remain in use and will have to be disposed of in the coming years as equipment reaches the end of its life. Because of their great stability, PCBs have proved to be among the most widespread and persistent man-made chemicals in the ecosystem. Furthermore, they accumulate in the fatty tissues of humans, fish, birds and other animals when PCB-contaminated food is eaten. The toxic and potentially carcinogenic effects of individual PCBs found in human tissues and breast milk are the subject of recent chemical investigations (Borlakoglu and Dils, 1991). Although PCB production has now ceased in most countries, and disposal by tipping and landfill methods has been replaced by new technologies including high-temperature incineration, there have been concerns about incomplete reduction to harmless products and especially the contamination of the environs of incineration plants by 'dioxins'. Improved analytical techniques, sensitive to low concentrations, have had to be developed to determine the presence of polychlorinated dibenzo-*p*-dioxins (PCDDs) and polychlorinated dibenzofurans (PCDFs) in soil, animal tissue and herbage (Hazardous Waste Inspectorate, 1986).

A further illustration of science serving technology is to be found in industrial contexts where the testing of materials by non-destructive methods is important. For example, aircraft manufacturers are continually seeking stronger, lighter and more reliable materials and means are needed of measuring and testing non-destructively how conditions of service effect these materials. A case in point is the testing of wear and tear on bearings which reduce the friction between the surfaces of rotating components in a gas turbine engine. The importance of such an apparently mundane operation is underlined when it is recognised that failed bearings, and other equipment subject to friction, cost US industry approximately US$40 billion a year; UK treasury estimates of annual savings to industry from the proper application of the principles of tribology (the study of friction and lubrication) are in the region of £4 billion at 1989 prices. When, in the mid-1980s, on a North Sea oil rig, a large articulated bearing failed, it resulted in total seizure of moving parts followed by fracture; part of the rig broke away and became a hazard to shipping. Its retrieval cost more than US$1 million (McLain, 1990).

A number of non-destructive techniques are available for monitoring bearing wear, including:

1 *Spectrometry*: appropriate when the metallic debris shed by worn bearings is very small in size (*c.* 1 μm in diameter). A sample of oil from the engine is heated, causing the metals in the debris to emit light of a characteristic wavelength. From this, the extent of bearing wear can be determined.
2 *Ferrography*: a technique suitable for use when dealing with larger metallic particles (*c.* 1–50 μm). Magnetic debris from lubricant samples is extracted and changes in particle type, shape and size are related to mode of wear.
3 *Magnetic chip detection*: magnetic chip collectors pick up debris from the circulating oil systems. The technique is sensitive to the larger size of particles associated with 'spalling', when pieces of metal tear away from bearings. The presence of such particles, about 200 μm in diameter, can be used to alert operatives that a bearing needs replacement or, in certain cases, to trigger the automatic shutdown of an engine or motor because wear has reached a dangerous level (McLain, 1990).

Perhaps nowhere is quality control of more direct importance for people than in the food industry. Northern Foods plc, a food manufacturer which supplies retail outlets such as Marks & Spencer, in a publication for sixth-formers describing the industry, used the example of freshly made sandwiches to illustrate the point.

> Consider the micro-biological implications of placing prawn, cucumber and tomato next to each other in bread and butter. Spores, bacteria and friendly growth media abound – which is fine if you eat your prawn sandwich fresh, say half an hour after it is made. But a food manufacturer has to make such sandwiches for sale in a store many miles away. The standard of hygiene in even the most scrupulously clean home kitchens wouldn't do. We need something more like a hospital operating theatre, with the goods then packed and transported at controlled temperatures to keep bacterial growth stable – because temperature control can only be truly effective if the dish to be controlled meets a bacterial standard at the start. Therefore technologists have to identify in advance the problems of a new recipe, analyze the hazards, preferably remove them from human control, but definitely design a no-fail bacterial count into the manufacturing process.
>
> (Northern Foods, 1988: 4–5)

It is clear that without scientific knowledge and techniques, such food manufacturing processes could not be developed. Indeed, Northern Food plc subtitles its publication *Chemical and Biological Science in the Future's Food Industry*.

'Doing science' and 'doing technology': process considerations

It has sometimes been argued that there is a general problem-solving process, the activities in which scientists and technologists engage being simply particular illustrations of this and having much in common. Table 5.1 summarises one such view of the relationship which was discussed at an Institute of Physics Conference on the interactions of physics and technology (Schilling, 1988: 19–20).

The implication is that mastery of the processes of 'doing science' will benefit those 'doing technology' not merely because systematic empirical enquiry will provide evidence which is of direct use, but, more significantly, because the processes

Table 5.1 Problem-solving processes

General model for problem solving	*Science process*	*Technology/design process*
Understand the problem	Consider a natural phenomenon	Determine the need
Describe the problem	Describe the problem	Describe the need
Consider alternative solutions	Suggest hypotheses	Formulate ideas
Choose one solution	Select one hypothesis	Select one idea
Take action	Experiment	Make product
Evaluate the product	Does result fit hypothesis?	Test product

themselves are very similar. Certainly, when the Interim Report of the Secretary of State's Working Group on Design and Technology was published in 1988, it drew critical comment from bodies such as the Secondary Science Curriculum Review (SSCR) and the Association for Science Education (ASE) because of an alleged overemphasis on the differences between the processes of science and technology. According to the ASE (1989: 53), many activities of science and technology in which pupils engaged at Key Stages 1 and 2 were identical. For the SSCR, the differences between

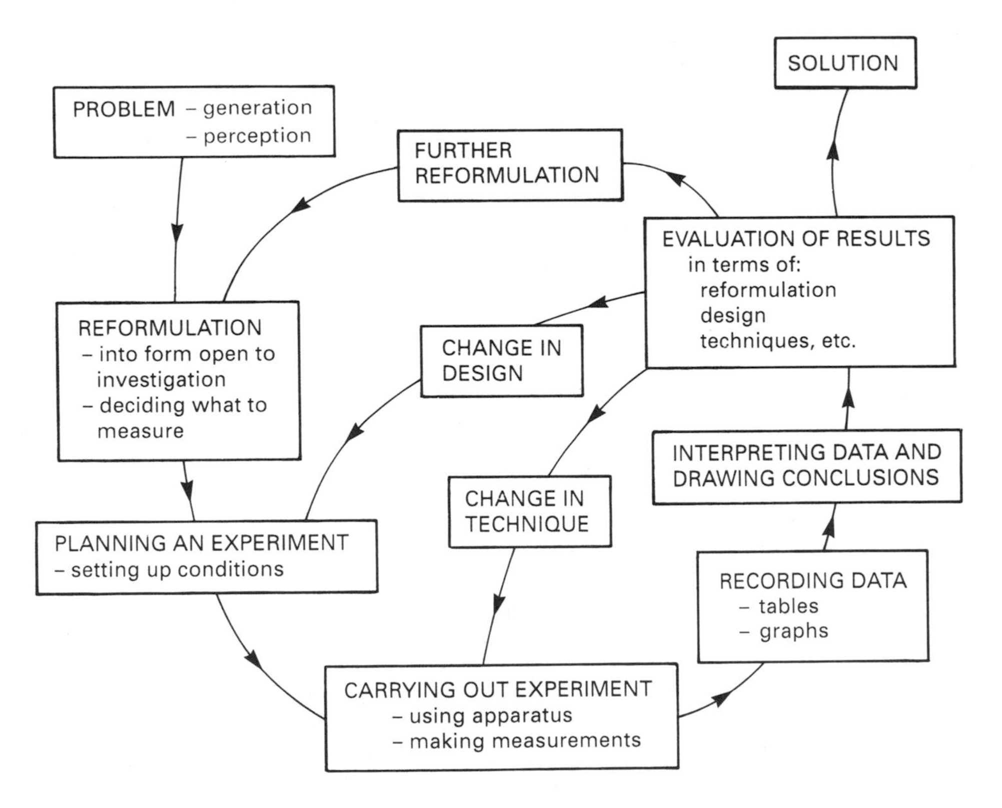

Fig. 5.1 The APU science problem-solving model.

science and technology reside not in the processes but 'in the nature of the purposes and products of the two activities' (SSCR, 1989: 14).

In order to explore further the extent to which 'doing science' is the same as 'doing technology', it is helpful to compare models of the processes which have some empirical foundations in observations of children working on science and technology problems (Figs 5.1 and 5.2). At first glance, it would seem that the two activities share several common features. Both are purposeful activities, both involve value judgements and both require the modelling of ideas and 'visionary thinking'. Furthermore, the descriptions of the activities employ common terms, such as 'generating a problem/detailing a problem', 'planning' and 'evaluation'.

Closer inspection reveals significant differences, however. For example, neither model says anything about the constraints under which the activities take place. The difference is well illustrated by the account of the biologist V. B. Wigglesworth FRS, writing in 1955 about the experience of pure scientists recruited to work on practical war-time problems:

> In the pure science to which they were accustomed, if they were unable to solve problem A they could turn to problem B, and while studying this with perhaps small prospect of success they might suddenly come across a clue to the solution of problem C. But now they must find a solution to problem A, and problem A alone, and there was no escape. Furthermore, there proved to be tiresome and unexpected rules

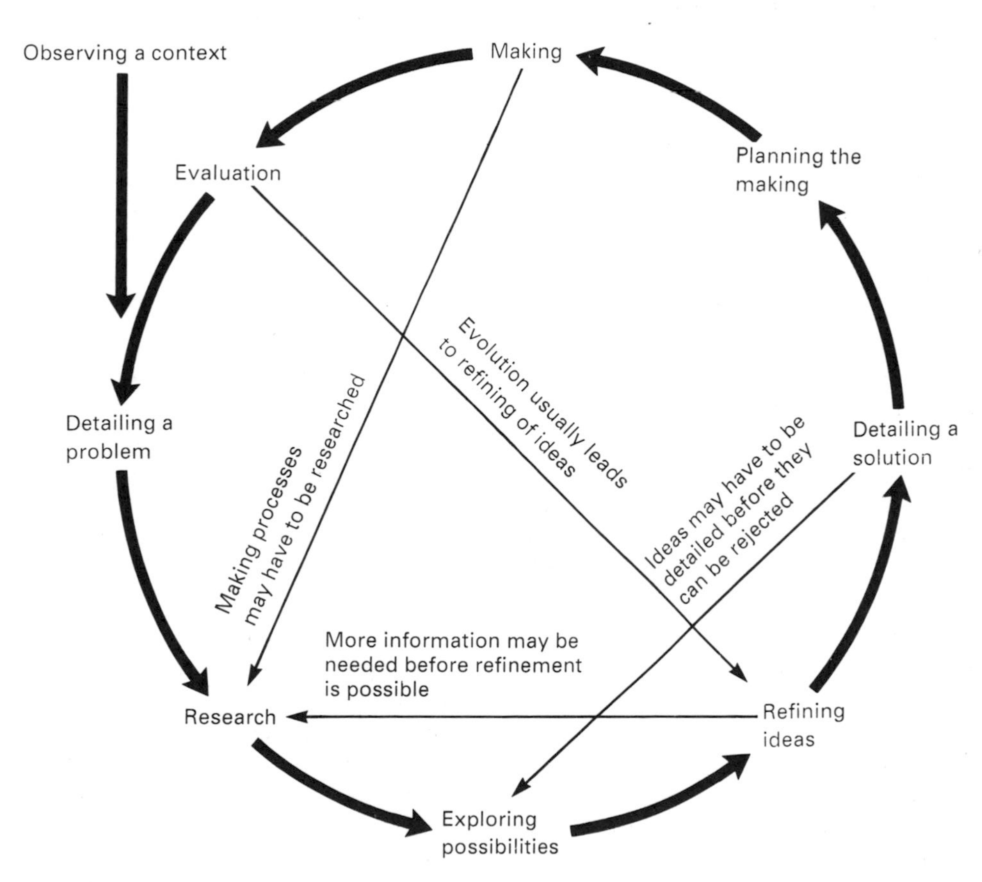

Fig. 5.2 An interacting design cycle.

> which made the game unnecessarily difficult: some solutions were barred because the materials required were too costly; and yet others were excluded because they might constitute a danger to human life or health. In short, they made the discovery that applied biology is not 'biology for the less intelligent', it is a totally different subject requiring a totally different attitude of mind.
>
> (Wigglesworth, 1955: 34)

The physical chemist Michael Polanyi FRS makes the same point in different words:

> In feeling his way towards new problems, in collecting clues and pondering perspectives, the technologist must keep in mind a whole panorama of advantages and disadvantages which the scientist ignores. He must be keenly susceptible to people's wants and able to assess the price at which they would be prepared to satisfy them. A passionate interest in such momentary constellations is foreign to the scientist, whose eye is fixed on the inner law of nature.
>
> (Polanyi, 1958: 178)

The point underlines that both the models under review, whilst they refer to 'evaluation', are silent on the criteria to be used. For science, if the theory or hypothesis 'fits the facts', if it does not breach the canons of good scientific practice (e.g. parsimony, replicability), then contextual preferences external to science play no part. In contrast, the products of technological activity have to satisfy diverse external criteria. Not only must the product 'work' (i.e. do what it was intended to do), but also it must satisfy a range of other conditions which may include environmental benignity, cost, aesthetic preferences, ergonomic requirements and market size. 'Doing science' is different, therefore, from 'doing technology', and to suggest that the processes correspond is misleading. It follows that expertise in 'doing science' is no guarantee of technological capability. The only qualification to add to this assessment is that, as described in the first section of this chapter, science comes in various 'shapes and sizes' (see p. 42), some of which – such as strategic and applied science – call into play external considerations which rarely afflict pure science. In these cases, the processes of 'doing science' and 'doing technology' draw closer. As mentioned earlier, however, these are not the varieties of science upon which most school science is modelled.

Operational principles and scientific knowledge

In embarking on the designing and making of any device (artefact, system or environment), a fundamental requirement is what Michael Polanyi has called *the operational principle* of the device. He means by this what would be embodied in a patent, i.e. a description of 'how its characteristic parts . . . fulfil their special function in combining to an overall operation which achieves the purpose' (Polanyi, 1958: 238). This is different from a statement of scientific knowledge. As Polanyi points out, patent law:

> . . . draws a sharp distinction between a *discovery*, which makes an addition to our knowledge of nature, and an *invention*, which establishes a new operational principle serving some acknowledged advantage . . . only the invention will be granted protection by a patent, and not the discovery as such.
>
> (Polanyi, 1958: 177)

The operational principle also serves to define a class of devices (e.g. clocks, cameras, microwave ovens, knitting machines), representatives of which all operate on the same principle. According to Polanyi, however, a knowledge of science 'would in itself not enable us to recognise' such a device (1958: 330). He uses the example of a team of physicists and chemists confronted by a grandfather clock and able to investigate it by all the scientific means at their disposal, without being able to refer to any operational principles. In these circumstances, they would not be able to conclude it was a clock because the questions 'Does this thing serve any purpose and, if so, what purpose, and how does it achieve it?' can be answered only by testing the device practically as a possible instance of known, or conceivable, machines. As Polanyi concludes, 'The complete (scientific) knowledge of a machine as an object tells us nothing about it as a machine' (p. 330) and 'the class of things defined by a common operational principle cannot be even approximately specified in terms of physics and chemistry' (p. 329).

It would appear that there are two distinct kinds of knowledge involved here, the technological and the scientific, with the former in no way dependent on the latter. Of course, once having recognised the device under investigation as a clock and gained some understanding of the way in which the different components function (e.g. there are weights whose fall under gravity provides the drive for the device; there is a pendulum whose regular period of swing controls the speed at which the clock works; there is an escape mechanism which is released by the pendulum swings; there are hands which turn to indicate the passage of time, etc.), it may be possible to use scientific knowledge and techniques to improve the working of the device. For example, its efficiency may be improved by reducing friction; its life extended by reducing corrosion or employing new materials. Also, such knowledge may be valuable in explaining malfunctions and failure. But scientific knowledge is of value only to the extent that it can be related to the operational principles of the device.

Although the operational principle has its origins outside science and cannot be derived as a matter of logical entailment from the body of scientific knowledge, there may be clues in the latter which help to suggest new operational principles and new classes of devices. Without knowledge of the properties and sources of infrared radiation, it would not have been possible to construct thermal-imaging cameras and develop the Forward Looking Infra-Red (FLIR) system used in air/sea rescues. Knowledge that atomic nuclei with an odd number of nucleons possess net spin and hence a magnetic moment which responds to the presence of a magnetic field underlies the development of the technique of nuclear magnetic resonance imaging, now widely applied in medicine. Designer molecules of new substances, such as Sucralose, Tate and Lyle's calorie-free sweetener, could not be made without a detailed understanding of the structure of organic substances and techniques for manipulating changes in functional groups of atoms, even though scientists do not have a theory to explain flavour and why some molecules produce a 'sweet' sensation in the mouth. The size of the development costs of a new sweetener for the world market today, estimated at in excess of £200 million (Cookson, 1991), is an indication that, although scientific knowledge may suggest new operational principles, its conversion into them is anything but a straightforward matter.

Scientific concepts and design parameters

Writing about the transfer of knowledge between science and technology, as evidenced by his detailed study of the origins of radio, Hugh Aitken concluded that:

> Information that is generated within one system exists in a particular coded form, recognisable by and useful to participants in that system. If it is to be transferred from one system to another – say from science to technology . . . it has to be translated into a different code, converted into a form that makes sense in a world of different values.
>
> (Aitken, 1985: 18–19)

In other words, the knowledge that is constructed by scientists in their quest for understanding of natural phenomena is not always in a form which enables it to be used directly and effectively in design and technology tasks.

An illustration may help to clarify this point. It has been estimated that water- and excreta-related diseases account for 80 per cent of all sickness in developing countries and are responsible for some 25 million deaths each year, with children being especially at risk. Biological approaches to the understanding of excreta-related diseases yield classifications in terms of their causal agents such as viruses, bacteria, protozoa and helminths. Whilst these are of value in treating the diseases, they do not readily assist the design of practical interventions and the application of limited resources which have as their objective the reduction of excreta-related infections.

Public health engineers have, therefore, had to

Table 5.2 Environmental classification of excreta-related diseases (from Feachem *et al.*, 1983)

Category	*Features*[a]	*Infections*	*Dominant transmission foci*	*Major control strategies*
I	Non-latent, low infectious dose (< 100 organisms)	Enterobiasis Enteric virus infections Hymenolepiasis Amoebiasis Giardiasis Balantidiasis	Personal contamination Domestic contamination	Domestic water supply Sanitary education Improved housing *Provision of toilets*
II	Non-latent, medium or high infectious dose (> 10 000 organisms), moderately persistent and able to multiply	Typhoid Salmonellosis Shigellosis Cholera Path. *E. coli* enteritis Yersiniosis *Campylobacter* enteritis	Personal contamination Domestic contamination Water contamination Crop contamination	Domestic water supply Sanitary education Improved housing *Provision of toilets* Treatment prior to discharge or re-use
III	Latent and persistent with no intermediate host; unable to multiply	Ascariasis Trichuriasis Hookworm infection Strongyloidiasis	Yard contamination Field contamination Crop contamination	*Provision of toilets* Treatment prior to land application
IV	Latent and persistent with cow or pig intermediate host; unable to multiply	Taeniasis	Yard contamination Field contamination Fodder contamination	*Provision of toilets* Treatment prior to land application Cooking of meat Meat inspection
V	Latent and persistent with aquatic intermediate host(s); able to multiply (except *Diphyllobothrium*)	Clonorchiasis Diphyllobothriasis Fascioliasis Fasciolopsiasis Gastrodiscoidiasis Heterophyiasis Metagonimiasis Paragonimiasis Schistosomiasis	Water contamination	*Provision of toilets* Treatment prior to discharge Control of animal reservoirs Control of intermediate hosts Cooking of fish and aquatic vegetables
VI	Excreta-related insect vectors	Bancroftian filariasis (transmitted by *Culex pipiens*), and all the infections listed in Categories I–III which may be transmitted by flies and cockroaches	Insects breed in various faecally contaminated sites	Identification and elimination of suitable breeding sites

[a] *Latency*: a latent organism requires some time in the extra-intestinal environment before it becomes infective to man. Persistency refers to the ability of an organism to survive in the extra-intestinal environment.

construct different types of classification better suited to their ends. One such is an environmental classification based on the environmental transmission pattern of the diseases (Table 5.2). Those infections in Categories I and II are due to agents such as viruses, protozoa and bacteria which can infect immediately after excretion, but which cannot survive for long outside a human host. The prevalence of such diseases suggests they are spread by direct faeco-oral transmission routes such as occur when people lack sufficient water for personal and domestic hygiene. A priority for their control, therefore, is the improvement of domestic water supplies, along with a programme of sanitary education. In contrast, infections in Categories III, IV and V are due to helminths which require some time outside their human host to become infective again and which can survive for extended periods in environments outside the human intestine. Control here would give a high priority to improved sanitation facilities (Mara, 1983: 48–9).

The essential point here is that design parameters do not always map neatly and precisely on to the parameters in terms of which scientific knowledge has been constructed. As Aitken deployment of available resources and the aims of associated health education programmes.

The essential point here is that design parameters do not always map neatly and precisely on to the parameters in terms of which scientific knowledge has been constructed. As Aitken noted, the latter has frequently to be reworked if it is to become of technological use. Making the same point differently, John Staudenmaier has argued that technological knowledge, possession of which empowers in the field of practical action and enables effective interventions in the made world, is not the same in form and sometimes in substance as knowledge produced by the basic sciences. It is knowledge which is structured by the tension between the demands of functional design on the one hand (i.e. it must enable some practical purpose to be achieved) and the specific constraints of the context of working on the other (i.e. it must satisfy externally imposed requirements such as the need to maintain environmental quality, to match the skills of available personnel and the characteristics of available materials and components) (Staudenmaier, 1985: 104). This integration of 'the abstract universality of a design concept and the necessarily specific constraints of each ambience in which it operates' would seem to be the primary cognitive problem of technological knowledge (Staudenmaier, 1985: 111) (see Fig. 5.3).

The contrast between the detailed specificity and design functionality of technological knowledge and the abstract generality and design-unrelated nature of scientific knowledge is well exemplified by consideration of the steam engine. For the practical task of designing and building a simple Newcomen engine which would deliver a specified amount of work in a particular context, decisions were needed about such variables as the diameter and length of the steam cylinder, the length of the piston's stroke and the number of strokes per minute. The construction of something like a stuffing-box, to prevent escape of steam whilst the piston was being driven upwards, at the same time permitting the piston rod to pass and re-pass, had to be accomplished. Some means of condensing the steam was necessary to allow the down-stroke of the piston and the resumption of the cycle. Preferably, as James Watt realised, this should not cool the cylinder and piston; otherwise, heat would be needed to restore their temperatures before steam could drive the piston upwards again. Safety and other valves would have to be designed and positioned and materials chosen for the construction of the various parts of the engine. These, and related considerations, were the pre-occupations of those who laboured to build steam engines that would enable water to be pumped from deep mines and, later, ships, railway engines and factory machinery to be driven.

All this was in sharp contrast to the concerns of Watts' younger contemporary, Sadi Carnot, across the Channel. Whilst Carnot was well aware of the social and economic significance of steam engines, he was critical of the level of understanding of them. It was his contention that:

> The phenomenon of the production of motion

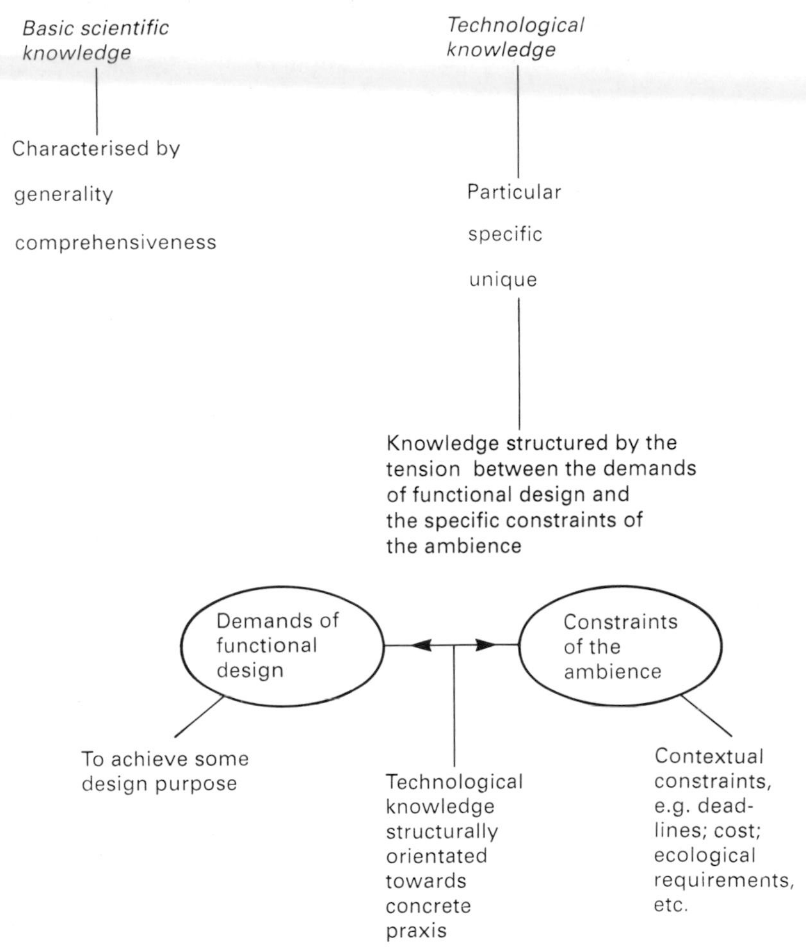

Fig. 5.3 Technological knowledge: Knowledge which empowers its possessors in the field of practical capability, enabling them to operate effectively in the made world.

> by heat has not been considered from a sufficiently general point of view . . . In order to consider in the most general way the principle of the production of motion by heat, it must be considered independently of any mechanism or any particular agent. It is necessary to establish principles applicable not only to steam-engines, but to all imaginable heat-engines, whatever the working substance and whatever the method by which it is operated.
>
> (Carnot, 1960: 6)

From his memoir, *Reflections on the Motive Power of Fire and on Machines Fitted to Develop that Power*, first published in 1824, it is clear that Carnot had an intimate knowledge of the construction and workings of heat-engines of many types. In the course of his argument, he discussed the advantages and disadvantages of engines using different 'elastic fluids' such as atmospheric air, alcohol vapour and steam, as well as solids and liquids. But practical considerations were transcended in his quest for general principles which would apply irrespective of the type of engine. These he established, though using the terminology of his age, including the concept of heat as a fine fluid called caloric. The conditions for the most effective possible operation of a heat-engine were that the working substance had the same temperature as the heat source at the beginning of its expansion and the same temperature as the condenser at the end. In other words, an engine of perfect efficiency would carry the working fluid through a complete cycle, beginning and ending with the same set of conditions.

Whilst the universality and insight of Carnot's theorising is remarkable – his memoir has been described as 'the most *original* work of genius in the whole history of the physical sciences and technology' (Cardwell, 1972: 129) – its very generality and abstractness made it of little immediate use to those constructing steam engines. Allowed one book from which to derive guidance on the building of a steam engine, few of his contemporaries or even later engineers, would have chosen Carnot's memoir in preference to other more practical books.

Carnot himself readily acknowledged the rarefied nature of his conclusions. In the final section of his work, when reviewing the ability of existing engines to make use of all the heat energy in coal burnt to raise the steam, he wrote:

> We should not expect ever to utilize in practice all the motive power of combustibles . . . The economy of the combustible is only one of the conditions to be fulfilled in heat-engines. In many cases it is only secondary. It should often give precedence to safety, to strength, to the durability of the engine, to the small space which it must occupy, to the small cost of installation, etc. To know how to appreciate in each case, at their true value, the considerations of convenience and economy which may present themselves; to know how to discern the more important of those which are only secondary; to balance them properly against each other, in order to attain the best results by the simplest means: such should be the leading characteristics of the man called to direct, to co-ordinate the labours of his fellow men, to make them co-operate towards a useful end, whatsoever it may be.
>
> (Carnot, 1960: 59)

This was a fine statement of the technologist's role in resolving considerations which were often conflicting. Whilst it is debatable whether 'thermodynamics owes more to the steam-engine than the steam-engine owes to thermodynamics', Carnot was clear that thermodynamics, the foundations of which he was laying, was a necessary though not sufficient resource for the building of useful engines. It needed to be integrated with other kinds of knowledge to realise its potential in the world of practical action.

It is sometimes the case that, as Staudenmaier asserted, technological knowledge is not only different in *form* but also in *substance* from scientific knowledge. The reworking of science for articulation with practical action may yield new formulations and concepts which are better adapted to the needs of technological activity. For example, data may be 'collapsed' to produce practical measures such as the UK National Energy Foundation's National Home Energy Rating (NHER: a 10-point scale). The aim here is to provide architects, builders and surveyors with a ready means to calculate the energy costs of a house, a score of 10 being indicative of high energy efficiency (Clover, 1990).

Further examples are to be found in engineering handbooks; the design requirements for mechanical building systems draw upon concepts such as 'effective sensible heat ratio' and 'ventilation cooling load', which find no place in academic physics texts. Interior lighting designers work with concepts such as 'discomfort glare' and 'disability glare'. From a different field, pharmacologists, for their particular purposes, do not categorise chemicals, as chemists do, in terms of molecular structures and functional groups. A more useful classification is according to human responses to the substances, e.g. stimulants, depressants, decongestants, analgesics, vasodilators.

The adaptation and reformulation of theoretical knowledge from science in order to produce technological knowledge have been the subject of recent research by historians of technology. One well-explored case is the invention and development of the AC induction motor in the closing decades of the nineteenth century. The work of men like Charles P. Steinmetz, the AC expert of the General Electric Company in the USA, involved departing from the classical Maxwellian electromagnetic theory in order to take account more effectively of energy losses caused by hysteresis, eddy currents and magnetic leakage, which determined the actual performance of motors. Maxwell's approach included a coefficient of self-induction which conflated both useful and leakage flux, so reducing its value as a design parameter. Steinmetz introduced new concepts such as 'leakage inductance' and 'primary admittance', which enabled more accurate calculations of motor performance to be made. He also derived an 'equivalent circuit' for the induction motor, which gave engineers a visual understanding of the physical relationships modelled in his mathematical equations and which aided design work (Kline, 1987).

Cathedral, quarry or company store?

Some of the ways in which science is an essential resource for the development of technological capability have been reviewed in this chapter. From its purest form – the cathedral dedicated to an adventure in ideas about the natural world – can be drawn methods of experimental and quantitative investigation and mathematical modelling procedures, tools of wide applicability. The cathedral is also the repository of the natural laws to which all technological devices must comply, as well as of newly discovered phenomena which can suggest novel and improved ways of tackling technological problems.

What is also apparent, however, is that technologists in their work can rarely specify in advance what items from the cathedral will prove to be of most use to them. For them, the cathedral has to be treated as a quarry, visited and revisited less to marvel at the beauty of the creations there than to search out those items which look as though they might be of use. Carefully wrought conceptual edifices may be raided, without regard to form and structure.

As we have seen, perhaps to protect the cathedral, workshops for science have been created where strategic and applied investigations predominate. The products of these go at least some way to providing technologists with what they seek, if not in shaping their needs. They also begin the process of adaptation and reformulation of pure science in order to make it more directly applicable in technological situations. To some extent, they may be seen as company stores where the products of the cathedral are reorganised and remodelled to make them more accessible to practical users rather than worshippers. The implications for the school curriculum of these various relationships between science and technology are clearly important and are the subject of the next chapter.

References

Advisory Council for Applied Research and Development (1986) *Exploitable Areas of Science*. London: HMSO.

Aikenhead, G. (1986) The content of STS education. *Missive to the Science–Technology–Society Research Network*, 2(3), 17–23.

Aitken, H. G. J. (1985) *Syntony and Spark. The Origins of Radio*. Princeton, N.J.: Princeton University Press.

Association for Science Education (1989) Response to the Interim Report of the National Curriculum Design and Technology Working Group. *School Technology*, 22(2, 3), 53–5.

Borlakoglu, J. T. and Dils, R. R. (1991) PCBs in human tissues. *Chemistry in Britain*, 27(9), 815–18.

Bybee, R. W. (1987) Science education and the Science–Technology–Society (STS) theme. *Science Education*, 71(5), 667–83.

Cardwell, D. S. L. (1972) *Technology, Science and History*. London: Heinemann.

Carnot, S. (1960) *Reflections on the Motive Power of Fire and Machines Fitted to Develop that Power* (translated and edited by R. H. Thurston). In E. Mendoza (ed.), *Reflections on the Motive Power of Fire*, pp. 1–59. New York: Dover Publications.

Clover, C. (1990) Heating takes a beating around the home. *The Daily Telegraph*, 23 July, p. 17.

Cookson, C. (1991) Rich treats in the sugar bowl. *Financial Times*, 12 September, p. 33.

Department of Education and Science (1988) *National Curriculum Design and Technology Working Group Interim Report*. London: DES and the Welsh Office.

Feachem, R. G., Bradley, D. J., Garlick, H. and Mara, D. D. (1983) *Sanitation and Disease: Health Aspects of Excreta and Waste Water Management*. Chichester: John Wiley.

Fensham, P. J. (1991) Science and technology education: A review of curriculum in these fields. In P. W. Jackson (ed.), *Handbook of Research on Curriculum 1991*. New York: Macmillan for American Educational Research Association.

Further Education Unit and the Engineering Council (1988) *The Key Technologies: Some Implications for Education and Training*. London: FEU.

Hazardous Waste Inspectorate (1986) *Hazardous Waste Management: 'Ramshackle and Antediluvian'?* Second Report. London: Department of the Environment.

Johnson, J. R. (1989) *Technology: Report of the Project 2061 Phase 1 Technology Panel*. Washington, D.C.: American Association for the Advancement of Science.

Kline, R. (1987) Science and engineering theory in the invention and development of the induction motor, 1880–1900. *Technology and Culture*, 28(2), 283–313.

Layton, D. (1988) Revaluing the T in STS. *International Journal of Science Education*, 10(4), 367–78.

Mara, D. D. (1983) The works and days of sanitation. *The University of Leeds Review*, 26, 45–57.

Mason, R. (1983) *A Study of Commissioned Research*. London: HMSO.

McLain, L. (1990) Systems to keep the ball rolling. *Financial Times*, 6 March, p. 18.

Northern Foods (1988) *The Most Useful Science: Chemical and Biological Science in the Future's Food Industry*. Norfolk: Thorburn Kirkpatrick.

Polanyi, M. (1958) *Personal Knowledge: Towards a Post-critical Philosophy*. London: Routledge and Kegan Paul.

Rothschild, Lord (1971) *The Organization and Management of Government R&D: A Framework for Government Research and Development*. Cmnd. 4814. London: HMSO.

Schilling, M. D. (1988) Science, Technology or Science and Technology. In The Institute of Physics, *Physics and Technology: Interactions in Education*, pp. 17–22. Bristol: Institute of Physics.

Secondary Science Curriculum Review (1989) Response to the Interim Report of the National Curriculum Design and Technology Working Group. *School Technology*, 22(2, 3), 13–17.

Senker, J. (1991) Evaluating the funding of strategic science – some lessons from British experience. *Research Policy*, 20(1), 29–43.

Smolimowski, H. (1966) The structure of thinking in technology. *Technology and Culture*, 7, 371–83.

Staudenmaier, J. M. (1985) *Technology's Storytellers: Reweaving the Human Fabric*. Cambridge, M.A. and London: MIT Press and Society for the History of Technology.

Wigglesworth, V. B. (1955) The contribution of pure science to applied biology. *Annals of Applied Biology*, 42, 34–44.

CHAPTER 6

Reworking the school science–technology relationship

At an international conference on science, technology and mathematics education in 1991, one science educator dubbed technology as 'the new kid on the curriculum block', adding that we needed to keep a careful watch on developments to see if the relationship with other subjects would evolve as 'bully or buddy', 'coloniser or collaborator'. Certainly, the inclusion of technology as a component of general education poses intriguing problems of curriculum organisation and interrelationships, to say nothing of content, pedagogy and assessment. In this chapter, some of these issues will be explored from the particular perspective of the relationship between science and technology. (More general consideration of the teaching and learning of design and technology is provided in other volumes in the series.)

Curriculum organisation

At least three broad approaches have been employed for the incorporation of technology in the curriculum of general education:

1 Technology as a distinct subject alongside other school subjects such as science and mathematics.
2 Technology across the whole school curriculum, all subjects contributing, to the extent they are able, to the development of children's technological capability.
3 Technology combined with science.

The justifications and implications of each of these approaches are reviewed below.

Technology as a separate subject

Theoretical arguments in support of this option invoke the nature of technological knowledge as a unique and irreducible cognitive mode. They likewise draw upon the integrative and holistic nature of design and technological activity in which purported stages such as identifying needs and opportunities or modelling cannot be kept uninfluenced by other 'stages' such as evaluating. It is also argued that in the past technology has too often been misunderstood or misrepresented, e.g. treated as 'merely applied science' or constrained by narrow vocational considerations. Only by allowing it to develop in its own curriculum space is it likely to fulfil its potential as a contributor to general education.

Of course, powerful practical considerations to do with staffing, accommodation, the timetable and other resources may also dispose a school to incorporate technology as a separate subject, whilst legislation and national arrangements for assessment of children's attainments, as in England and Wales, can clearly exert a major influence.

Separateness does not equate with self-sufficiency, however, and as we have seen in previous chapters, science is not only an essential resource for the development of technological capability, but fulfils this role in multifarious ways.

Careful negotiation of a mutually fruitful relationship between school technology and school science is, therefore, of critical importance. For science teachers, the essence of the problem is how to provide a science education which assists children to develop progressively a view of the natural world as scientists have constructed it, whilst at the same time servicing the needs of children engaged in specific technological tasks. To build the cathedral and simultaneously man the company store is a challenge which is both new and daunting.

Fortunately, some at least of the components of the cathedral require little change. Facility in the use of experimental methods and ability to draw upon a broad and general understanding of scientific phenomena are prime resources for technological activities. There may be practical problems of timing and co-ordination, the technologist requiring a knowledge of, say, enzyme chemistry or electromagnetic induction before the science teacher has planned to deal with these topics. Self-learning packages and the use of educational technology could be of some assistance here. The past history of service teaching (e.g. mathematics for science students), however, suggests that when the service subject is unable to make the necessary adjustments, for whatever reasons, the attractions of independence become irresistible and responsibility for the teaching is assumed by the other partner. One consequence here is that there may be duplication of teaching effort with pupils experiencing different approaches to the study of topics such as electronics and mechanics, according to whether they are in science or technology lessons.

Whether this should be a matter for concern is debatable. Much turns on whether the different approaches are seen as betokening conflict or as productive outcomes from a symbiotic relationship. In support of the latter view, our new understanding of the nature of technology and of technological knowledge does suggest that much academic science needs to be reworked to make it articulate effectively with design parameters in specific practical tasks. We lack experience at school level of the kinds of transformations needed, but some simple examples might help to suggest what is often required (Layton, 1990).

1 *Adjusting the level of abstraction*
A science teacher, aiming to develop an understanding of the kinetic–molecular theory of heat, might deal with the conduction of heat through materials in terms of molecular motion. For the technologist, engaged in the task of improving the insulation of a building and reducing heat losses, a simple fluid flow model of heat might be adequate for most work.

Similarly, a designer of lighting and electrical power systems for a new building will be unlikely to work with a model of electric current as a charge cloud of electrons migrating over the nuclei of copper atoms.

Again, whilst a proton donor model is a powerful means of understanding the acidic properties of materials, it is over-complex for most everyday situations involving acids. Generalising, what is implied here is the need for the technology student, having reached an understanding of science at a high level of abstractness, to be able to climb back down the ladder of abstraction and judge where to stop, i.e. recognise which level is most appropriate for a specific technological purpose.

2 *Repackaging knowledge*
The 'problems' which people construct from their experiences do not map neatly on to existing scientific disciplines and pedagogical organisations of knowledge. What is needed for solving a technological problem may have to be drawn from diverse areas of academic science at different levels of abstraction and then synthesised into an effective instrumentality for the basic task in hand. The student who designed and made a swimming aid for use by mentally and physically handicapped children had to bring together knowledge of the properties of various materials, concepts from physics such as density and principles such as that of Archimedes, an understanding of the muscular, physiological and anatomical characteristics of users, as well as the conditions for them to feel confident and secure in water.

3 *Reconstruction of knowledge*
This involves creating or inventing new 'concepts' which are more appropriate than the scientific ones to the practical task being worked upon. The adoption of practical units, as opposed to scientifically based ones, illustrates what is involved here. Examples have already been given in the previous chapter of instances where technologists have found it necessary to devise concepts which are more effective than academic scientific ones in the specific circumstances of their work.

4 *Contextualisation*
Science frequently advances by the simplification of complex real-life situations; its beams in elementary physics are perfectly rigid; its levers rarely bend; balls rolling down inclined planes are truly spherical and unhampered by air resistance and friction. Decontextualisation, the separation of general knowledge from particular experience, is one of its most successful strategies. Solving technological problems necessitates building back into the situation all the complications of 'real life', reversing the process of reductionism by recontextualising knowledge. What results may be applicable in a particular context or set of circumstances only.

The examples above do not exhaust the possibilities, but we might summarise the general position as follows. Much recent research on children's learning of science has been premised on a view of learning as a process of knowledge construction which starts from the prior knowledge – preconceptions, intuitions, alternative frameworks – that students bring to their lessons. Consideration of the relationship between science education and technology education suggests an additional process is important (Fig. 6.1). This involves the deconstruction and reconstruction of the scientific knowledge acquired, in order to achieve its articulation with practical action in technological tasks (Layton, 1991).

Technology across the curriculum

The rationale for this approach derives from a view of technology as a complex human activity which cannot adequately be practised and understood if immured within a limited timetable slot. Its resources and ramifications involve many components of the curriculum of general education. For example, consideration of whether a problem is appropriately tackled as a design and technology activity (e.g. fitting a lever arm on the kitchen tap of an elderly lady whose hands are crippled by arthritis; controlling the behaviour of disruptive prisoners by chemical means) or as a socio-economic/political one (e.g. altering the ways in which a society treats its elderly infirm members or its criminal offenders) could be a valid concern of social studies or history lessons. Similarly, unless the 'hidden curriculum' of a school – its general ethos, reward systems, organisational practices,

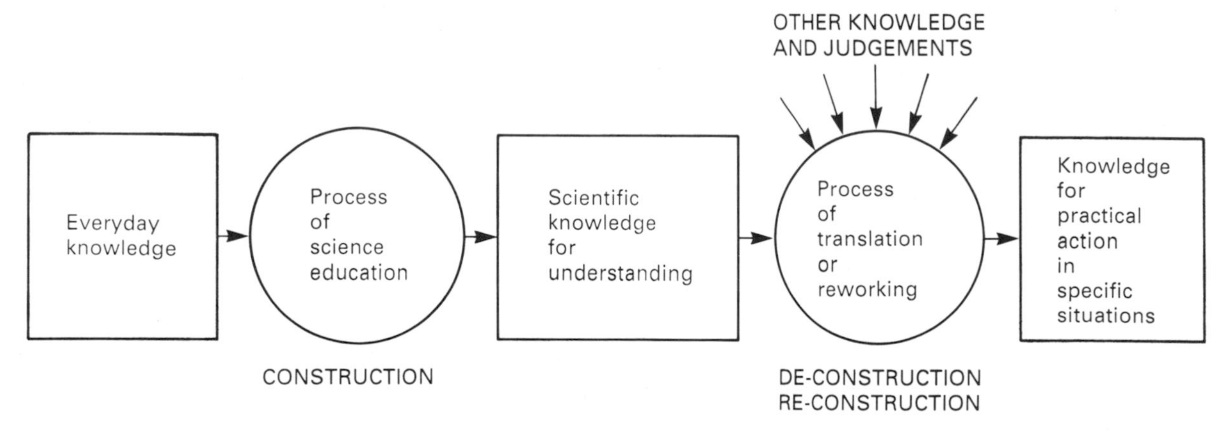

Fig. 6.1 Construction and de-/re-construction of scientific knowledge.

resource distributions – testifies to the high status of practical knowledge, as well as academic learning, then it is unlikely that the full potential of technology in the curriculum of general education will be realised. It is important to emphasise here that the term 'practical' is not used in any sense as antithetical to 'intellectual'. From what has gone before in earlier chapters, it will be clear that the capabilities which a technological education fosters involve intellectual abilities of a high order.

The implication here is that the inclusion of technology in the curriculum of general education entails a change in the culture of schools. It is not that the existing culture, with whatever emphasis this might have on academic achievements and pastoral concerns, needs to be displaced. Rather, it requires enhancement by the celebration of practical capability as an extension of scholastic attainments into the wider world of purposeful design and action.

Implementation of 'technology across the curriculum', however, frequently leads to dismemberment of the unitary concept of 'technological capability' as embodied, for example, in the 1990 Order for Technology in the National Curriculum of England and Wales. In this connection, it is interesting to look at a significant report from an Association for Science Education Technology and Science Working Party under the chairmanship of Brian Woolnough (ASE, 1988). This asserted that technology should be 'an integral part of every pupil's liberal education', its organisation being 'according to a whole school curriculum policy set in the context of a largely common curriculum'. Four distinct but interrelated strands of technology education were identified as components of the formal curriculum, the whole to be supported by a school ethos which regularly encouraged technological activities. The four strands were:

1 *Technological literacy*, defined as familiarity with the content and methodologies of a range of technologies
2 *Technological awareness*, meaning awareness of 'the personal, moral, social, ethical, economic and environmental implications' of technological developments.
3 *Technological capability*, meaning here the ability to tackle a technological problem, 'both independently and in co-operation with others'.
4 *Information technology*, interpreted as pupils' 'competence and confidence in the technological handling of information'.

In primary schools, it was expected that all the strands would be developed 'not through "subjects" but through integrated, interdisciplinary, investigational topic work'. In secondary schools, whilst a distinct subject, technology could be the means by which technological literacy and technological capability were fostered, technological awareness 'should be developed in the context of most subjects and areas of study; through history, geography and English as well as through the sciences'. Information technology, likewise, 'should be taught as an integral part of different subjects' and it was judged that for technological capability 'the most effective approach will necessitate a more interdisciplinary structure'.

The ASE report made clear that the four strands were not intended to represent a 'sequential hierarchy' and that their ordering was not significant. In this respect, they differ from components of technology education in a transatlantic attempt to devise a taxonomy of capacity for technological decision making (Todd, 1991: 271):

Levels	*Types of knowledge*	*Competence*
1 Technological awareness	Knowledge that	Understanding
2 Technological literacy	Knowledge that	Comprehension
3 Technological capability	Knowledge that and how	Application
4 Technological creativity	Knowledge that and how	Invention
5 Technological criticism	Knowledge that, how and why	Judgement

Whilst this analysis of technological decision making is suggestive, no empirical evidence in support of the taxonomical claim is provided. Also, the scheme is not related directly to considerations of curriculum organisation or, specifically, to the contributions of different school subjects.

A third attempt to describe components of technology education uses the notion of functional competencies (Layton, 1987: 4.5). It distinguishes between:

1 Technological awareness or *receiver competence*: the ability to recognise technology in use and acknowledge its possibilities (e.g. recognise what a word processor might be able to do for you in your workplace).
2 Technological application or *user competence*: the ability to use technology for specific purposes (e.g. use a word-processor to edit text).
3 Technological capability or *maker competence*: the ability to design and make.
4 Technological impact assessment or *monitoring competence*: the ability to assess the personal and social implications of a technological development.
5 Technological consciousness or *paradigmatic competence*: an acceptance of, and an ability to work within, a 'mental set' which defines what is a problem, circumscribes what counts as a solution and prescribes the criteria in terms of which technological activity is to be evaluated.
6 Technological evaluation or *critic competence*: the ability to judge the worth of a technological development in the light of personal values and to step outside the 'mental set' to evaluate what it is doing to us (e.g. it might be encouraging a view of social problems in terms of a succession of 'technological fixes' rather than more fundamental considerations).

It is clear that several of the competencies could be developed in different subjects of the curriculum of general education and that the later competencies clearly move the study of technology in the direction of moral education.

A less ambitious and more practically focused listing of abilities was included in the Interim Report of the Secretary of State's Working Group on Design and Technology (DES, 1988: 17–18). Design and technological capability was stated to include all of the following, at least:

- pupils are able to use existing artefacts and systems effectively;
- pupils are able to make critical appraisals of the personal, social, economic and environmental implications of artefacts and systems;
- pupils are able to improve, and extend the uses of, existing artefacts and systems;
- pupils are able to design, make and appraise new artefacts and systems;
- pupils are able to diagnose and rectify faults in artefacts and systems.

Whilst the Terms of Reference of the Working Group required the members to bring forward proposals for the programmes of study and attainment targets of a subject called technology, they were instructed to assume that pupils would draw on knowledge and skills from a range of subject areas, 'but always involving science and mathematics' (pp. 86–7).

These attempts to identify discernible strands or components of technology education raise a question about their mutual independence. Clearly, it is possible to use a technological artefact (a motor car, a refrigerator, a videotape recorder) effectively without necessarily being able to diagnose and rectify faults in it. Depending on the component abilities identified, some degree of independence seems possible. However, the issue arises in its sharpest form when considering whether it is possible to 'design and make' effectively without drawing upon knowledge and insights derived from the critical appraisal of the personal, social and other implications of technological developments. In terms of the categories in the ASE report, can technological capability be developed independently of technological awareness, and vice-versa? The 1990 proposals for technology in the National Curriculum of England and Wales eschewed the notion of 'awareness' as a separable component of technology education, regarding what was covered by this heading as integral to the development of design and technological capability. A cross-curricular approach to school technology which assumes that contributions to the development of pupils' technological 'awareness' will come from several subjects is left with a major problem of co-ordination and of re-uniting in pupils' minds and activities the considerations which interact in the practice of technology.

As for the role of science in a cross-curricular approach to school technology, the ASE report argued that:

1 Science teachers' expertise in electronics, computing, home economics, biotechnology and industrial methods enables them to contribute to the development of pupils' technological literacy.
2 In so far as science is taught in its social, economic and environmental contexts, considering the applications and implications of science, pupils' technological awareness will be enhanced.
3 Similarities between 'the technological process' and 'science as a problem-solving activity' reinforce aspects of technological capability. Also, scientific knowledge gained from science lessons is a vital resource for solving technological problems.
4 Familiarity by pupils with the use of computers in science lessons will build confidence in the use of information technology.
5 Science teachers can enhance the technological ethos of a school by clubs, competitions, visits, industrial experience, displays and exhibitions.

Whilst this acknowledges the contribution of science as clearly significant, even allowing for differences of opinion about similarities between the processes of scientific investigation and those involved in undertaking technological tasks, comparable lists could be made for other school subjects, such as geography and history, and the uniquely symbiotic character of the relationship between science and technology is not affirmed. Perhaps even more importantly, it would seem as if school science could enter into a new relationship with school technology without itself undergoing any significant change. The existing good practices of school science are surveyed and drawn upon in support of technology education. It has been a major contention of this book that the negotiation of a relationship between school science and school technology is more complex than this. It constitutes a challenge to school science which entails an inescapable measure of change.

Technology combined with science

There are several versions of the case for incorporating technology in the curriculum of general education by combining it with science. It has been argued, for example, that 'to put undue emphasis on technology as a subject, to promote its definition, is to stifle the wider role for science education' which has been 'gaining pace around the world' (Holbrook, 1992: 8–9). This wider role is associated with science curricula that are context-based, and that give prominence to applications and implications. The contributions of science and technology to both the creation and solution of social problems tend to feature strongly and students engage in decision-making activities.

Reviewing the variety of such STS courses, Fensham (1988: 353–4) has distinguished between:

1 Science-determined courses in which the sequence of the science knowledge is identical to that in traditional disciplinary science education, with the STS material added on;
2 Technology-determined courses in which the science content is determined by its relation to the technology or the socio-technological issue being studied; and
3 Society-determined courses in which the science and technology to be studied are determined by their relevance to the particular societal problem under consideration.

The concern is that the introduction of technology as a separate subject in the curriculum, alongside science, would usurp crucial elements of these courses and debilitate the STS movement. Far better, the argument goes, to build on the intimate relationship between science and technology, and consolidate the goals of scientific understanding and design and technology capability in one combined course.

A particular version of this general proposition concerns the place of electronics in the school curriculum. According to Lewis (1991: 1):

> . . . any approach which places too much emphasis on the structure and characteristics of specific [electronic] devices suffers from two major drawbacks. The first is that these devices are likely to be of only transient importance (witness valves, or indeed transistors). Secondly, not enough time will be left over to provide experience of designing and building electronic systems to perform useful tasks. The latter is vital if students are to acquire some appreciation and understanding of the power of modern electronics, of its role in technology, and of its influence on human societies.

An alternative to the traditional device-centred approach was pioneered by the Nuffield Advanced Physics project, which developed a systems approach using conceptual building blocks (logic gates, bistables, astables, counters, etc.) which had some durability in the face of rapid developments at the level of devices. Thc cxtcnsion of this approach to earlier levels of physics teaching, enabling electronics to become an integral part of physics courses, would, in Lewis' judgement, 'do nothing but strengthen physics as a school subject'. At the same time, it would present it in a way which more accurately reflected the activities of most of the world's physicists today.

Such moves by science educators to assimilate technology into science courses prompt questions about motives and the extent to which technology is being cast in an instrumental role in order to enhance interest and attainment in science. There is nothing morally reprehensible about such tactics, provided children are not being sold short and denied experience of modes of thought and action that are uniquely technological. As noted in Chapter 5, we so far lack well-tested examples of courses that successfully promote both scientific understanding and technological capability.

A quite different argument for combining technology with science in general education is associated with countries where demographic and economic considerations make the addition of a new subject to the curriculum impossible. In Zimbabwe, for example, as in many African countries, the population is expanding faster than the economy, secondary school enrolments have increased ten-fold since Independence in 1980, and there is an acute shortage of well-qualified and experienced science teachers. Although the benefits of technological capability have been well recognised (Carelse, 1988; Robson, 1989), human and material resources are such that there is no prospect of developing a new technology curriculum for schools. Instead, a technology-oriented science syllabus was adopted covering themes such as Science in Agriculture, Science in Industry, Science in Structures and Mechanical Systems, Science in Energy Uses and Science in the Community.

In a review of deliberations and papers from the World Conference on Education for All at Jomtien in 1990, Knamiller (1992: 288–9) deploys a similar argument:

> . . . the major message to emerge is the need for 'operacy', educating children and adults to operate effectively in daily life, at the workplace and in the community. . . This necessitates a process-oriented curriculum related to everyday life. . . Technology education, reported to be virtually absent from school curricula around the world, is also process-oriented for the purpose of cultivating problem-solving, creative and entrepreneurial skills. As these new curricular thrusts are holistic, problem-solving, action-oriented and interdisciplinary, they need not be forced as separate subjects into already overloaded curricula. Science and maths remain, but as lattices through which processes are woven, e.g. forces and materials for designing machines, sums and spread sheets for engaging the market.

The image is appealing, though the feasibility of using science in this way for the development of technological capability (operacy) is questionable. Processes cannot be extracted from or woven into content and context quite so easily as seems implied. Moreover, there are practical obstacles, such as large class sizes (Knamiller cites rural primary school classes of 191 and 205 children in Malawi) and lack of materials, which militate against the learning of process skills for practical action.

Even so, and particularly at the secondary school level, a number of developing countries have reconstructed their science syllabuses to make them relate more effectively to contemporary personal and national needs. In Botswana, for example, where water is always in short supply, where solar energy appliances are becoming increasingly common, where the bicycle is a standard form of transport and where primary health care, especially in relation to intestinal infectious diseases, is of paramount importance, an integrated science programme for the two years of junior secondary school was devised. Each of the topics mentioned in the previous sentence featured as a unit of study with the Botswana Technology Centre, the Renewable Energy Technology Project, the Department of Water Affairs, the Water Hygiene Project, the Mines Department and other national agencies serving in advisory capacities (Nganunu, 1988). Similar indigenous developments have occurred in the Philippines (Tan, 1988) and Nigeria (Jegede, 1988; Ajeyalemi, 1990). A question remains, even so, about the extent to which such courses empower students for practical action, however effectively they might illustrate the relevance of scientific principles to everyday life. Knowledge of the relationships is no guarantee of intent to act, much less a substitute for the technological know-how necessary to achieve a desired outcome in the made-world. As Hines and Hungerford (1984: 127) have reported in the field of environmental education, 'knowledge alone, while significantly correlated with responsible environmental action, is not sufficient to predispose individuals to attempt to remediate environmental problems'. Practical capability has crucial conative, no less than cognitive, components, and perhaps the confidence to intervene and act can only come through repeated experiences of success from personal involvement in technological tasks.

Organisational futures

What follows from this brief review of approaches to the incorporation of technology in the curriculum of general education? First, it is important not to formulate the problem as one of either/or: for example, *either* separate subject technology *or* technology across the curriculum. To do so is to misrepresent the challenge. We might adapt here Karl Popper's (1972: 266) dictum that:

> Whenever a theory appears to you as the only possible one, take this as a sign that you have neither understood the theory nor the problem which it was intended to solve.

and say

> Whenever a specific technology curriculum appears to you as the only possible one, take this as a sign that you have neither understood the nature of that curriculum nor the educational purpose it was intended to achieve.

Indeed, a mixed economy may be a fruitful way forward for many schools, with a curriculum subject called technology *and* contributions from a range of other subjects, not least science, all within a school culture positively supportive of practical capability, as the ASE report suggested. The seamless web view of technology suggests that successful learning will depend on a broad base of diverse experience which can only be provided by a whole curriculum in which the relevant activities are pervasive and integral. Technology education is perhaps best seen as emblematic of that wider radical transformation of mission which schools are presently undergoing and to which reference was made in Chapter 1.

Second, the situation in developing countries provides a salutary reminder of the power of context in determining what is possible in organisational and other terms. The attempts to clone specific models of technology education being developed in the (relatively) resource-rich North are sensibly being resisted. Also, we should be careful not to write off alternative models from the South as necessarily inferior versions; as we have come to realise in science education, the North has often much to learn from the South, not least in the areas of informal and non-formal education, if only it will allow its eyes to see.

Third, and perhaps most crucially, it will be important to avoid a situation in which science education and technology education confront each other as competitors. It is perhaps understandable that science education, which has been criticised for failing to capture the imaginations and energies of many students, e.g. in the USA and the UK, should view the arrival of technology on the curriculum scene as potentially threatening. There have even been suggestions that traditional disciplinary science should be reserved for a minority, with technology becoming the staple of the majority in mass educational systems (Chapman, 1991). Opposition between school science and school technology would be destructive to both subjects, as well as a negation of the symbiotic relationship that sustains them in industrial and other research and development contexts.

On the other hand, effective partnerships rarely occur spontaneously; there must be benefits in the relationship for each participant, and these will only become clear after detailed and shared exploration of each other's territory to determine how best they might collaborate. It has been the purpose of this book to contribute to this exploration which is presently taking place in many schools and elsewhere, as in discussions between subject teaching associations such as the ASE and DATA. Many practical issues of finance, accommodation, material resources and pedagogy will need to be negotiated in establishing the relationship; for the most part, these have been judged outside the scope of the book, the prime focus of which has been the nature of the two activities, science and technology. A complementary agenda of importance would address questions such as whether the science to be used by students performing technology tasks should be provided on 'a need to know' basis or should be 'front-end loaded', i.e. science taught formally, with perhaps some opportunities to use it in problems and different contexts prior to embarking on the technology task. The debate about this particular issue has been well summarised by Cooper (1989).

It has also been the case that the emphasis in previous chapters has been on the ways in which science education might serve the needs of technology education, but it should be affirmed that benefits flow in the other direction also. Some indication of these was provided in the sections above describing the ways in which science education has moved in the direction of technological applications, both as contexts for the understanding of scientific principles and as illustrations of how science relates to action in industry and everyday life. A closer association of school science and school technology could bring other benefits to science also. The articulation of science with practical action would help to project a more authentic view of the nature and creative foundations of scientific knowledge. It would encourage recognition of both the tacit, craft contributions to the generation of this knowledge (Ravetz, 1971) and the fact that, if it is to form the basis of action, it 'often has to be reshaped, refashioned and contextualized in ways that allow its integration with other kinds of knowledge, beliefs and judgements that are often personal and markedly context bound' (Jenkins, 1992). This outcome could be seen as a major contribution to the humanising of a subject which many school students presently see as providing little room for personal interpretation and judgement. Revealing the templates and techniques by means of which the cathedral was constructed, and perceiving it as itself a technological artefact, may also go some way to assisting it to function as the company store.

References

Ajeyalemi, D. (1990) *Science and Technology Education in Africa. Focus on Seven Sub-Saharan Countries*. Lagos: University of Lagos Press.

Association for Science Education (1988) *Technological Education and Science in Schools*. Report of the Science and Technology Sub-Committee. Hatfield: ASE.

Carelse, X. F. (1988) Technology education in relation to science education. In D. Layton (ed.), *Innovations in Science and Technology Education*, Vol. 2, pp. 101–12. Paris: UNESCO.

Chapman, B. R. (1991) The overselling of science education in the eighties. *School Science Review*, 72(260), 47–63.

Cooper, S. (1989) Technology across the curriculum and its impact on science teaching. *Education in Science*, 135, November, pp. 10–11.

Department of Education and Science (1988) *National Curriculum Design and Technology Working Group Interim Report*. London: DES and the Welsh Office,.

Fensham, P. J. (1988) Approaches to the teaching of STS in science education. *International Journal of Science Education*, 10(4), 346–56.

Hines, J. M. and Hungerford, H. R. (1984) Environmental education: Research related to environmental action skills. In L. A. Iozzi (ed.), *Summary of Research in Environmental Education 1971–82*. Monographs in Environmental Education and Environmental Studies, Vol. 2. Columbus, Ohio: ERIC Clearing House for Science, Maths and Environmental Education.

Holbrook, J. (1992) Science and technology education – a vital link. Unpublished paper prepared for the ICASE Seminar, Weimar International Technology Education Conference, April.

Jegede, O. J. (1988) The development of the science, technology and society curricula in Nigeria. *International Journal of Science Education*, 10(4), 399–408.

Jenkins, E. W. (1992) Knowledge and action: Science as technology? In R. McCormick, P. Murphy and M. E. Harrison (eds), *Teaching and Learning Technology*. Reading, M.A.: Addison-Wesley in association with the Open University.

Knamiller, G. (1992) Review of *Education for All: Purpose and Context. Roundtable Themes 1*. Paris, UNESCO, 1991. *Science, Technology and Development*, 10(2), 288–9.

Layton, D. (1987) Some curriculum implications of technological literacy. In *Paper 1: Papers submitted to the Consultation held on 15 and 16 November 1985*, pp. 4–8. York: St. William's Foundation Technology Education Project, 5 College Street, York Y01 2JF.

Layton, D. (1990) *Inarticulate Science?* Occasional Papers No. 17. Liverpool: University of Liverpool Department of Education.

Layton, D. (1991) Science education and praxis: The relationship of school science to practical action. *Studies in Science Education*, 19, 43–79.

Lewis, J. (1991) *Electronics Teacher's Guide*. Science and Technology Education Document Series No. 40. Paris: UNESCO.

Nganunu, M. (1988) An attempt to write a science curriculum with social relevance for Botswana. *International Journal of Science Education*, 10(4), 441–8.

Popper, K. (1972) *Objective Knowledge: An Evolutionary Approach*. Oxford: Clarendon Press.

Ravetz, J. (1971) *Scientific Knowledge and its Social Problems*. Oxford: Clarendon Press.

Robson, M. (1989) Introducing technology through science education. Case Study 2: Zimbabwe. In World Bank/British Council, *Educating for Capability: The Role of Science and Technology Education*, Vol. 2. London: The British Council.

Tan, M. C. (1988) Towards relevance in science education: Philippine context. *International Journal of Science Education*, 10(4), 431–40.

Todd, R. (1991) The changing face of technology education in the United States. In J. S. Smith (ed.), *DATER 91*, pp. 261–75. Loughborough: Department of Design and Technology, Loughborough University of Technology.

CHAPTER 7

Responses and resources: a review of the field

In this final chapter some responses by those in schools to the problem of negotiating a mutually supportive relationship between technology and science will be reviewed. A number of projects working at the interface of technology and science have produced curriculum materials and otherwise supported developments in this area. Whilst the chapter draws heavily on these helpful materials and permission to do so is gratefully acknowledged, the examples discussed make no pretence of comprehensive coverage and, in any case, the field is far from static.

An example from school X

School X, a secondary school with a strong commitment to the development of technology education, organised a 'great egg race' as a competition involving ten other similar schools. Each school entered a team of four students, usually two boys and two girls, drawn from years 8 to 10 (i.e. 13–15 year olds, with most students from the upper years). None of the students had previous knowledge of the task they would be asked to undertake, although all had demonstrated a keen interest in design and technology activities in their own schools.

The competition was sited in a hall with balconies on the first floor. Two parallel copper wires had been stretched from one side of the hall to the other, the ends being secured at the top of the railings on the balcony. On the ground floor, in the centre of the hall and directly under the mid-point of the parallel wires, a metal waste paper basket was situated. Teams were to construct a device which would transport a raw egg and deposit it in the waste paper basket without breaking the shell. The teams had to make their attempt from a position on the balcony at one end of the parallel copper wires and were not permitted to move from that position while trying to place the egg on the target. The egg was the only object to be left on the target area.

A list of materials and components was provided for the teams (see Table 7.1). All items on the list were priced; for certain items there was a limit on the number which a team could purchase. A notional budget of £1000 was available to each team and no materials other than those provided, or bought from the stores, could be used. The device constructed to transport the egg had to weigh no more than 1 kilogram and the attempt to place the egg on the target had to be completed in less than 5 minutes from the moment of launch from the balcony.

A data sheet offered suggestions to team members for methods of quick construction of a lightweight wooden frame to which axles and wheels could be attached, but competitors were free to develop other means of transporting the egg, if they so wished. The materials and components available for purchase placed some limits on the range of solutions which could be explored. For example, it would not have been possible to build a cantilever device from which to lower the egg; nor were extendible tongs a possibility because materials from which to construct them were not available. Three hours of working time were allowed to the teams for designing, constructing and testing, as well as for producing a set of drawings to show their ideas, the development of the design and the final solution adopted.

In the event, every team chose to construct some form of four (or six) wheeled buggy supporting a pulley over which string passed, one end being under the control of a team member and the other end being attached to a device to carry and deposit the egg. The wheels were positioned on the copper wires, relying on an indentation in their circumferences to hold them in place. The transporter was propelled by an electric motor with, in all but one case, direct drive to the wheels by means of a rubber band. The plan was to transport the buggy to the mid-point of the wires, then lower the egg into the waste paper basket and operate the release mechanism.

Despite much ingenuity in the design and construction of egg holders and dropping mechanisms, only one team succeeded in depositing the egg unbroken on target. Indeed, this was the only attempt out of those made by the eleven teams which landed an egg anywhere near the target area.

Table 7.1 Items for purchase by competitors

Items	*Price (£)*	*Maximum allowed*
Large motors	500	1
Small motors	200	2
Plastic discs	10	–
Straws	10	–
Micro switches	20	2
Push button switches	10	2
Springs	10	–
Nuts and bolts	10	–
String (thin)	5/m	–
String (nylon)	2/m	–
Stiff wire	10/m	–
Wire	10/m	–
Double sided tape	10/m	–
Masking tape	5/m	–
4 mm dowel	20/length	1
Cotton reels	5	–
Rubber bands	2 each	–
Welding rod	20/length	–
Wheels	10 each	–
10 mm sq wood	10/length	1
Gears	5	–
Pulleys	5	–

In talking to competitors about the way in which they were going about the task a number of interesting points emerged. Asked whether they had found science helpful in assessing what was needed to accomplish the task, or in analysing reasons for failure in trials, the universal response was negative. The problem had been conceptualised in terms which did not go beyond a common sense appreciation of it and an intuitive feel for what might work. In the discussions amongst students in their teams, when debating how best to tackle the problem, there was little reference to scientific principles or ideas. When the motor failed to propel the vehicle along the copper wires (and few vehicles got as far as a metre beyond the starting point, even with manual encouragement), there was no attempt to analyse the forces at work, only a contention that a 'larger motor' might be needed. The winning team was the only one to incorporate a gear box between the electric motor and the wheels. Two teams did weigh the egg before designing their vehicle and dropping mechanism, but in general quantitative considerations were not prominent in the thinking of the competitors.

There are many criticisms that can be made of 'egg-race' type of activities; for example, competitors are faced with someone else's problem, not one they themselves have defined and over which they have some sense of ownership; the task is often artificial and contrived, lacking a clear connection with everyday concerns; and the range of solutions is limited, even partially prescribed, by whatever resources are made available. Leaving these considerations aside, however, there are some important lessons to be learnt from the particular activity just described.

The prospect of success would have been enhanced if competitors, prior to settling on a design, had attempted to model the physical forces acting on the vehicle when mounted on the copper wires and carrying the suspended egg. Estimates of the magnitudes, directions and effects of these forces could have brought home to competitors, for example, the need for a low centre of gravity of the vehicle in order to reduce the risk of slipping off the wires, a common cause of disaster. Similarly, some rough quantitative estimate of the motive power to ensure forward progression in a controlled manner would have guided competitors in the choice of electric motor and the most appropriate mode of driving the wheels of the vehicle. Preliminary trials of the unloaded vehicle often indicated a lack of friction between the wheels and the wires; some knowledge of science could have helped to solve this problem. Possibly time constraints and the competitive atmosphere induced the students to adopt 'cut and try' intuitive strategies; certainly, there was little evidence of systematic experimental investigation in the development of their vehicles and the dropping mechanisms.

In Chapter 5, some ways in which science could serve as a resource for the development of technological capability were reviewed. One fundamental contribution of science was as a source of operational principles for technological developments. In this example of a 'great egg race', variations on the egg depositing mechanism were common, although few were consciously derived from scientific principles. There were, for example, no pneumatic devices. Most were simple mechanical solutions involving tipping or rolling of the egg after the container had landed on the base of the target. In actuality, few were ever put to the ultimate test because their transporting vehicles failed to travel sufficiently far along the wires.

As for the transporters themselves, there were no alternatives to the vehicle on wheels travelling on top of the wires and powered by a small electric motor. The wires from the motor to the power source on the floor of the balcony, of necessity some 4 metres in length, tended to become entangled with the longer length of string running over the pulley to the egg-dropping mechanism. No team explored, either on paper or in practice, the feasibility of an under-slung transporter, the design of which might have enabled a greater spatial separation of the motor and the dropping mechanism, so reducing the risk of snarl-ups. The extent to which available materials and components constrained operational principles is exemplified by the absence, even in the sketches of students, of consideration of alternative energy sources such as steam, compressed air or elastic bands. Similarly, competitors remained in thrall throughout to the parallel copper wires. No one contemplated, even to reject the idea, aerial passage from the balcony to the target by, for example, a large helium filled balloon. Likewise, subversive measures, such as slackening a copper wire to yield a catenary with its lowest point just above the target (not prohibited – or at least not referred to – in the printed rules of the competition), remained unexplored.

The purpose of this brief evaluation of one 'egg race' is not to criticise the students or their teachers. Many of the latter, if asked to relate the task to work in science lessons, would no doubt provide more and richer examples than those above. The central point is that the way in which students had been experiencing technology in their schools, all of which aspired to some excellence in this field, did not appear to have disposed them to reflect, as a matter of habit and because experience had testified to the benefits, on the ways in which scientific knowledge and skills might enhance their designing and making.

Science as a source of operational principles

The Science and Technology in Society (SATIS) 16–19 project of the Association for Science Education was set up in 1987 to provide teaching resources for students in the 16–19 age range. It built on the experience of an earlier SATIS project for 14–16 year olds and was intended to support general education and to enhance specialist science courses in academic and vocational programmes. Although not written specifically for technology students, some of the units have a design and technology orientation, although they do not always involve construction. There is an associated reader entitled *What is Technology?*

Unit 2 of the 16–19 project is described as an 'icebreaker'; its focus is the apparently simple task of emptying a bucket of water and it is usually undertaken as a group activity. Confronted by a plastic bucket full of water, students are invited to consider ways of emptying it. Suggestions may include:

- tipping the bucket over;
- making a hole in the bucket;
- drop bricks or other large insoluble objects into the bucket to displace the water;
- pour in an immiscible liquid which is more dense than water;
- hang a hook in the water, freeze the water and then lift out the water as a solid lump of ice;
- ladle out the water with a utensil such as a cup or saucepan;
- drop in a chemical, such as sodium, which reacts with the water violently and decomposes it;
- drink the water;
- use a length of pipe to siphon off the water;
- use a pump;
- use a sponge repeatedly, putting it in the water and then squeezing it out;
- use two electrodes and a battery to electrolyse the water, decomposing it into gaseous products.

Embodied in these suggestions are numerous physical and chemical principles. Thus, without some knowledge of change of state it would not be possible to design a solution to the problem which involved freezing. Similarly, unless students knew something of the process of electrolysis of water, the operational principle of decomposing the water into hydrogen and oxygen would not be available to them. While the list includes some suggestions of dubious validity, it by no means exhausts the possibilities; for example, biological approaches to the task are not well represented.

Having elicited a range of possible ways of tackling the problem, the unit then suggests that some practical constraints are introduced such as:

- the bucket cannot be touched or damaged;
- health and safety considerations, i.e. the method adopted must not be hazardous or injurious;
- cost; the method used must not be prohibitively expensive;
- time; a time limit for completion of the task can be imposed.

In the light of these, the suggested methods are reviewed and some are eliminated. Although the unit does not require students to use the operational principle they favour in the actual design, construction and testing of a device to empty the bucket, some practical work is incorporated. Density measurements of various liquids, and of foams, might be made in order to select an appropriate substance if that route is being followed. Optimum conditions, including surface area, air-flow rate and temperature, for the evaporation of the water might be investigated. The unit also suggests investigations into the working of a lavatory cistern, as a widely used mechanism for emptying a container of water in a controlled way. It would seem possible to use an adapted version of the unit with students younger than 16–19 in order to illustrate how science can be a rich source of operational principles for the solution of technological problems. Selection of an operational principle is, of course, only a first step in the technological task and its translation into an effective technological device will raise design and constructional problems which may even entail reconsideration of the principle chosen.

Making use of science and technology (MUST)

Both examples so far considered – the egg race and the bucket of water to be emptied – whilst illustrative of certain aspects of the relationship between school science and school technology, do not relate directly to real-life situations. In contrast, the MUST project, located at the Chemical Industry Education Centre, York University, has produced units of work for use with 13–16 year olds,

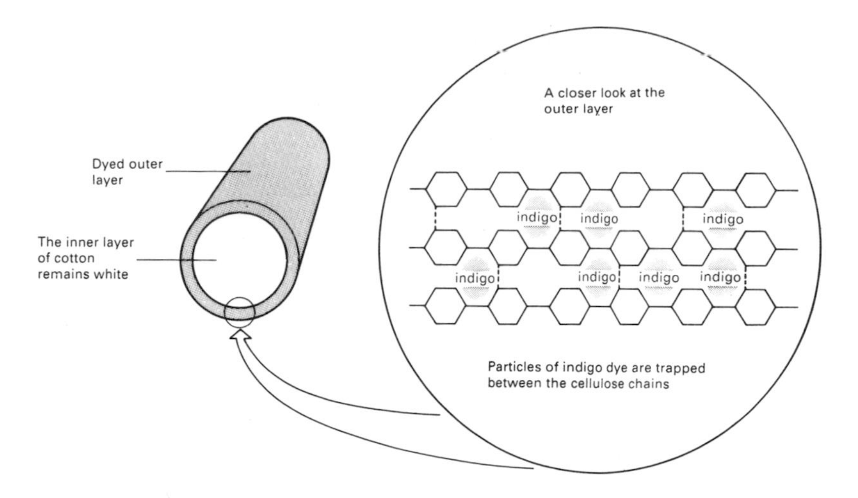

Fig. 7.1 Cotton thread dyed with indigo.

all of which are based on some situation or problem in an industrial context.

One typical unit, with an obvious and direct appeal to young people, is entitled 'Wearing Jeans'. Its subject is the method of producing denim, from which jeans are made, which has the faded appearance so fashionable in recent years.

Denim is a woven cotton fabric. For the manufacture of blue jeans, threads which have been dyed with synthetic indigo are used for the warp, whilst undyed cotton threads are used for the weft. Chemically, cotton is almost pure cellulose, a material made up of long parallel chains of glucose molecules. In the process of dyeing, particles of indigo become physically trapped between the chains in the fibres on the outside of the cotton thread. The indigo is not chemically bonded to the cotton and does not penetrate below the outer layer of a thread (Fig. 7.1). With wear and washing, over an extended period, the indigo dye is released from the surface of the threads and the denim assumes the faded look that has been so popular with young people.

In order to achieve this effect in newly manufactured jeans, the traditional method was to stone-wash, i.e. abrade the surface of the dyed cotton threads by tumbling the jeans with pieces of pumice stone in a large washing machine (Fig. 7.2). There are many disadvantages with this procedure. Pumice stones are costly to import and handle. Their abrasive action on the jeans can damage seams and hems, as well as the washing machine. Dust from the stones makes it necessary to introduce an extra wash for the denim, so increasing production time and costs; the dust cannot be disposed of by normal drainage and has to be transported by road to waste disposal sites, again putting up costs. Even after the extra wash, tiny fragments of pumice can remain in the jeans and could be dangerous to young children if ingested; time and labour are needed to remove this material.

Having provided an interesting account of the stone-washing process and its limitations, the unit now reveals an alternative means of fading the denim which depends on a chemical knowledge of cellulose. The new operational principle derives from the fact that the enzyme cellulase, produced by micro-organisms, is able to break down cellulose. If treated with cellulase under appropriate conditions, blue denim will fade because the cellulose chains on the outside of the cotton fibre are split up into simple sugar molecules and the trapped indigo particles are released. A scientific understanding of the effect of dyeing denim with synthetic indigo and a knowledge of the chemistry

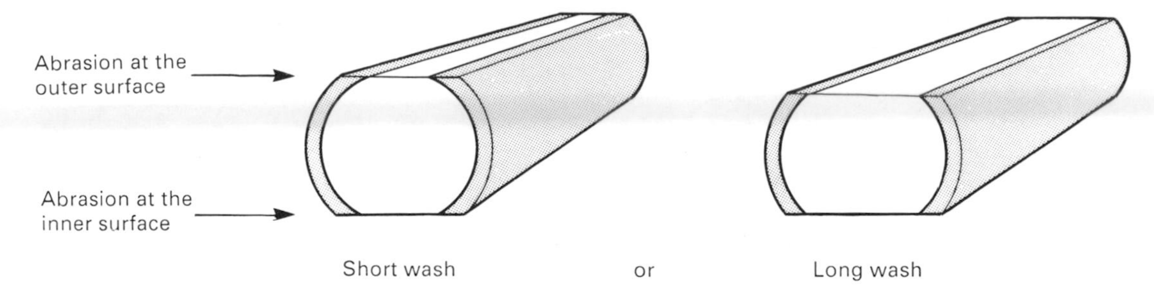

Fig. 7.2 'Fading' by abrasion.

of cellulose thus yields the means of producing faded jeans of improved quality, with reduced pollution and risks to children and, hopefully, lower manufacturing costs.

Other aspects of the process are covered by the unit, such as the removal of the starch size applied to cotton fibres to reinforce them, so reducing the risk of breakages due to mechanical strain in manufacture of the denim fabric. Enzyme chemistry is again involved.

From the standpoint of developing technological capability, the unit stops short of requiring students to design and make anything, although details are provided for the construction from plastic bottles of a model washing machine to demonstrate the enzyme-fading process. However, the recommended practical activities are largely concerned with establishing the conditions for the most effective treatment of the denim by cellulase (e.g. optimum reaction temperature, minimum period of treatment), for working safely and for reinforcing students' knowledge of chemistry (e.g. the specificity of enzymes, the structure of cellulose) and of the fruitful interaction of science and technology.

All this is important and valuable and, as with other units of the MUST project, science and technology are situated in contexts which are likely to interest many students. In terms of technology the seamless web, as portrayed in Chapter 3, and the intimate relationship between technology practice and values, as argued in Chapter 4, the unit presents a partial story only and leaves scope for further development if technological capability is the goal. On the specific issue of the relationships of science and technology, the science involved is brought to bear upon the technological problem without significant change in its character. There is little hint of the kinds of transformations discussed in Chapter 5 which assist its articulation with design parameters although the unit provides an excellent illustration of science as a resource for new operational principles.

The Science with Technology Project

Of projects in the UK perhaps that which most directly confronts the relationship between science and technology in schools is a joint venture of the Association for Science Education and the Design and Technology Association. The Science with Technology Project is aimed at students in the 14–19 years age range and the curriculum materials it produces are intended to become part of the ASE SATIS publications.

The project literature spells out the mutual benefits of collaboration between science and technology. For technology, there is the recognition and illustration that science provides knowledge and skills needed by students, alongside other resources, to develop technological capability. The project aims to provide materials which enable students to acquire scientific skills and knowledge in a way that makes them useful in design and make tasks. Also authentic and authoritative information from industry is used to provide contexts for these tasks. For science, there are resources which set scientific activities in context, develop investigative skills and build on the motivation that results from involvement in design and technology activities through relating the science to the process of designing and making in response to human need.

The project has identified three levels of support from and collaboration with science. There is, first, what it calls *essential science*, knowledge and skills which are so firmly embedded in the technological task that a successful outcome is impossible without them. In the MUST project on Wearing Jeans, a knowledge of the chemistry of cellulose and of the action of the enzyme cellulase could be regarded as essential science. Second, there is *useful science*, in the sense that this science facilitates the achievement of the technological goal. The ability to design an experimental investigation to determine the optimum temperature for the reaction between cellulase and cellulose would be an example of useful science. Finally, the project identifies opportunities to develop *further work in science* which builds on the relevance of the technological task and the motivation resulting from it. This work would be undertaken within the science programme of study as a positive spin-off from the technology activity. The MUST project, for example, includes experimental work as extension studies designed to reinforce students' appreciation of the highly specific nature of enzyme activity and the fact that cellulase has no action on the polyester threads used to sew up the jeans.

The resources developed by the Science with Technology Project are based on the model shown in Fig. 7.3. A common context is used to set tasks in both technology and science. Even so, the success of a partnership between technology and science clearly requires collaboration between departments and colleagues in a school in order to overcome a number of severe practical problems. First, there is no single mandatory body of scientific knowledge for design and technology activities. Especially if pupils are themselves identifying problems or are being faced by open-ended tasks, it is difficult to see how it is possible to front-end

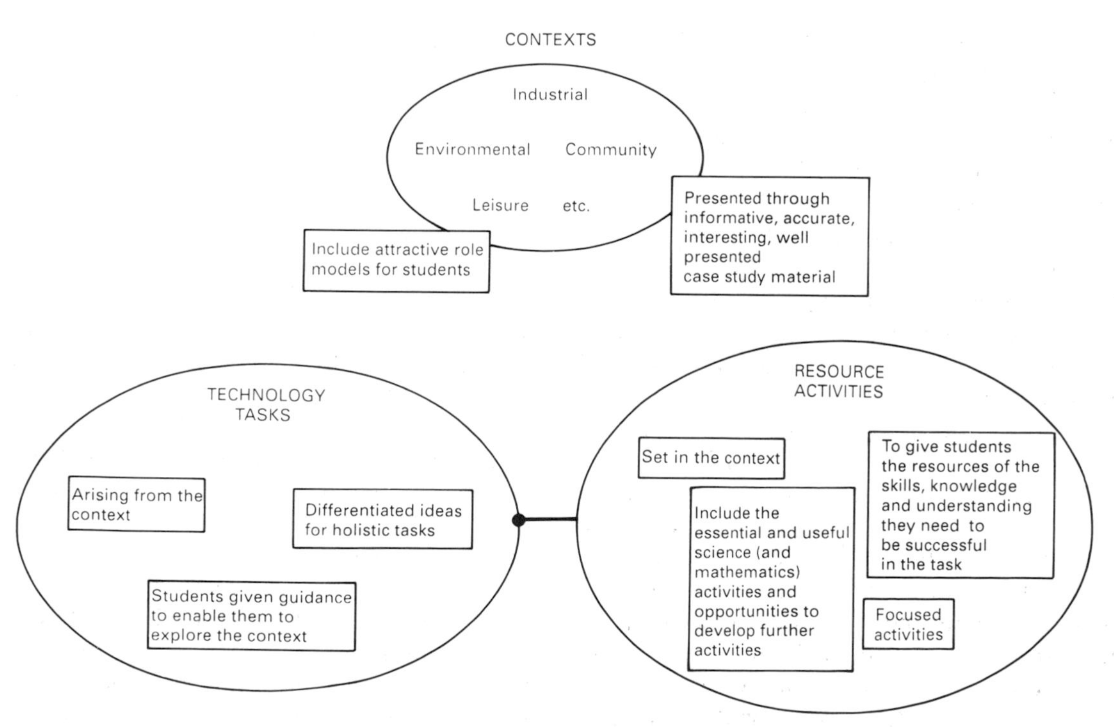

Fig. 7.3 The model used by the Science with Technology Project to develop resources.

load with scientific knowledge, pre-judging the science they are likely to need, without at the same time influencing the definition of the problem and encouraging closure on the type of solution to be adopted. If pupils are working on the reduction of accidents from reversing lorries, and this activity is prefaced by lessons on optics, it will not be surprising if optical solutions predominate, although solutions depending on other branches of science are clearly possible.

A second difficulty is that the need may arise in science and technology activities for scientific knowledge well before it is encountered in science lessons. As the report of an evaluation of the pilot phase of the Technological Baccalaureate commented, technology 'makes promiscuous use of [scientific knowledge], with no regard for the convenience of those concerned with designing coherence and progression into a programme of study for science' (Young and Barnett, 1992: 18). In other words, the external requirements of the subject being serviced may not correspond to the internal requirements of the discipline providing the service.

Third, and more fundamentally, even if science is accessible to students at the times in their design and technology activities when they need it, as we have seen not all scientific knowledge as provided in science lessons is in a form which makes its use in technological activities a straightforward matter. In the chemistry programme nutrients may be classified and studied as carbohydrates, proteins and fats, together with micronutrients such as vitamins and mineral sources of elements such as iron and iodine. The biology programme may deal with issues such as digestion, absorption and excretion. For the chef, designing and cooking a dinner, whilst the contribution from science would be a consideration, design parameters of a different kind would be paramount. Foods would be categorized according to how long they take to cook; whether to be served hot or cold; flavour; consistency; colour; need for preservatives, thickeners and texturisers etc. A different vocabulary and a different frame of reference would be called into play. The translation and integration of scientific knowledge about nutrients into culinary and dietary practice exemplifies the third practical difficulty of establishing a mutually fruitful relationship between school science and school technology.

The extent of collaboration between teachers of science and of technology is seen by the Science with Technology Project as possible at a number of different levels. In some situations it may be feasible and desirable to aim for fully *integrated work* in a course, a project or a task. In other contexts, *collaborative work* may involve the organisation of a coherent programme of study for students, the separate subjects retaining their identity and autonomy, with work being passed from one teacher and lesson to the next in order to provide coherence and continuity. Different again, the project identifies *co-ordinated work*, possibly with a common context for the different activities in the different subjects. Whilst this does not entail an overall coherent programme of study for students, they are encouraged to make connections between lessons or topics. Fourth, collaboration may be pitched at the level of *awareness* of what is going on in other subjects so that cross-references can be made and links indicated to students. Clearly, some combination of these levels of collaboration may also prove workable.

Ways forward

It is clear that there are no simple and general solutions to the problems confronting those who attempt to establish a productive relationship between school science and school technology. Certainly in the early stages, schools will need to work out their own way forward in the light of their particular circumstances – the geography of departments and resources, the history of inter-faculty collaboration in the school, the nature of personalities involved and the quality of infrastructural support, to mention only a few of the determinants. Whilst some degree of collaboration between science teachers and technology teachers is important, it is essential to be clear about the goals of the collaboration.

An understandable and defensible first move would be to look down the list of scientific knowledge and skills in the school's science syllabuses in order to identify those elements which seem to relate most directly to technological activities which might be undertaken. The proposals for the revision of attainment targets and programmes of study for design and technology in the National Curriculum (Secretary of State for Education and the Secretary of State for Wales, 1992) now include numerous cross-references to the Statutory Order for Science and, in one of the few journal articles on using science in design and technology, Dr David Barlex, a director of the Nuffield Design and Technology Initiative, has argued that a first place for technology teachers to look should be the Statutory Order for Science in the National Curriculum (Barlex, 1991: 149), preferably with science colleagues who can help in the matching of the level of statements of attainment to pupils' ability.

Barlex recommends that this exploration of the science curriculum should then be coupled with a revisitation of some familiar design and technology tasks. He uses the example of designing a nut cracker to show how an approach from the standpoint of the 'force' or 'energy' required to crack a particular kind of nut can lead to a physical modelling of the task and contribute to a technical specification for the device. Of course, this is only an initial step in the process. It is followed by investigation of ways of applying the required force (e.g. levers, screw thread) and of delivering the necessary energy (e.g. falling weights, ballistic pendulum, compressed spring). In the light of the results, an operational principle for the nut cracking device is chosen and design considerations relating to ease of use, pleasing appearance, selection of materials with appropriate behavioural characteristics and manufacturability are called into play. At all stages, decisions can be informed by scientific knowledge and skills, the extent of this being related to the age and experience of students.

One lesson to be drawn from this example has been well expressed by Professor M. J. French in a fascinating book, *Invention and Evolution. Design in Nature and Engineering* (1988: 300). He writes that

> The mind of the designer should be like a rich, open soil, full of accessible resources, of which the chief is an ordered stock of ways and means, illustrated by many examples . . . [This 'design repertoire'] should be organised on the most abstract lines practicable, so that any item in it is likely to be recalled in as many contexts as possible.

Others who have studied invention as a cognitive process endorse this view. Detailed reconstructions of the ways in which significant and successful inventors have achieved their goals show that not only do they build up and draw upon a personal 'design repertoire', but within this they have favoured means of achieving particular technological ends. These serve as a hallmark of their capability and a testament in their products to the identity of the designer (Carlson and Gorman, 1990; Gorman and Carlson, 1990).

One important goal of collaboration between teachers of science and technology, then, is the identification of the science which might assist not only the achievement of effective outcomes, but also the build-up of a repertoire of design and constructional resources, illustrated in multiple contexts. This has implications for the choice and control of the tasks on which students will work. A balance will need to be struck between prescriptive tasks, intended as opportunities to make use of particular taught scientific knowledge and skills, and more open-ended tasks which encourage lateral thinking and imaginative raids upon a student's expanding repertoire of technological 'ways and means'. The Nuffield Design and Technology Project makes a similar distinction between the kinds of tasks on which students will need to work. *Resource tasks* are ones which are designed to help pupils acquire the knowledge, understanding and skills necessary for capability in design and technology. *Capability tasks* are designed to provide pupils with opportunities to develop and demonstrate capability in design and technology. In the words of a project newsletter:

> Capability tasks without the underlying foundation provided by resource tasks will reduce pupils to

> operating on little more than heightened common sense. Resource tasks do not teach pupils to be capable. Good design and technology teaching will be based on the interplay of these two sorts of task. By choosing a sequence of capability tasks with associated resource tasks, teachers will be able to develop a design and technology curriculum that is right for the pupils in their school.
>
> (Nuffield Design and Technology Initiative *Newsletter* 2, 1992)

The approach to collaboration between teachers of science and those of design and technology by identifying scientific knowledge and skills in the science programmc which might be useful to design and technology students whilst clearly valuable, nevertheless leaves important problems unaddressed. Some of these are practical and organisational, such as how to plan the teaching to achieve maximum synergy. Solutions here are probably particular and context specific. Others, and notably the effective articulation of scientific concepts with design parameters (as discussed in Chapters 5 and 6), appear not to have been acknowledged, much less explored, in the projects and materials currently available. The judgement from this brief review of the field, admittedly limited to some UK resources only, must be that whilst the attempt to bring school science and school technology into a fruitful relationship has been started, and progress made, the analysis of the problem has so far not been taken far enough. 'Applying science' is not a simple matter of selection followed by routine use; the process is an active one which often entails the creative reworking of the science. As W.J.M. Rankine, Regius Professor of Civil Engineering and Mechanics at Glasgow in the nineteenth century and a distinguished pioneer of the use of science in technological tasks, expressed it, 'the application of these [scientific] principles to practice is an art in itself' (Rankine, 1857: 13).

Appendix: ASE policy statement on technology

1 Introduction

The Association for Science Education believes that Science and Technology are inextricably interwoven. For this reason, it is important to develop the relationship between the two, but not to deny the distinctive features or the separate identity of either. Science, like art, home economics, history and other subject areas, can make a contribution to the technological education of all pupils. In primary schools, the development of learning is encouraged by a thematic approach, which should automatically link science and technology with each other and with other subject areas. In secondary schools, technological education should be developed by supporting as many aspects of technology as possible. This might be achieved by the sequencing of science curriculum topics to match the needs of technology, by cross-curricular activities or by the presence of a science teacher on the technology teaching team.

2 The rationale for technological education

Technological education should form an integral component of the educational experience of all young people aged 5 to 19 years. As a consequence of this experience and that obtained in other subject areas, students will be better prepared to develop an awareness and an appreciation of the world and its cultures and the influence of past, present and future technological change.

Initially, young pupils should be encouraged, and helped to identify tasks in familiar contexts, which they are able to complete by drawing upon their present knowledge, understanding, experience and skills. In doing this, and in following other tasks sensitively introduced by the teacher, students will develop and extend their technological capability until they become self-sufficient, independent of the teacher and able to identify 'needs and opportunities'. In time, they should have sufficient confidence to generate, evaluate and present their own designs and acquire higher order skills in order to fulfil a particular task. As a consequence of this progressive development in their technological activities and abilities, young people will be enabled to play an active part in the control of their own environment and encouraged to participate in its positive development for those less fortunate than themselves. The development of technological literacy and capability will also provide many young people with relevant and appropriate preparation for adult life and employment.

3 Entitlement

- All pupils should receive a broad, balanced, progressive and appropriately co-ordinated technological education from 5 to 16 years of age. This technological education should continue post-16, but some specialisation is to be expected at this stage of education.
- Technological education should enable pupils to develop their technological ability through opportunities to take part in activities of an extended nature which take advantage of knowledge, understanding and skills from many areas of the curriculum.
- Information Technology is one aspect of Technology which should be an integral part of the learning experience of all pupils, at all stages, and in many areas of the curriculum.

Some projects concerned with the relationship between science and technology

Making use of Science and Technology

Project Officer: Terry Hilton, Chemical Industry Education Centre, Department of Chemistry, University of York, Heslington, York YO1 5DD. Telephone: 0904 432523.

Units include: Wearing Jeans; Fit to Drink; Frozen Assets; Captains of Industry; Hydrogen as an Energy Carrier; Recycling Cities; War against Pests; Sweet Success; What a Gas?; Magnox.

The materials are intended for use with 13–16 year olds. The activities are based on the practices and processes of industry.

Science and Technology in Society

The SATIS projects are initiatives of the Association for Science Education, College Lane, Hatfield, Hertfordshire AL10 9AA. Telephone: 0707 267411.

SATIS 14–16, the original project, includes 120 units. SATIS 16–19, for older students, comprises a flexible bank of resources designed to support general education and to enrich specialist science courses. A total of 100 units is supported by three readers entitled *What is Science?*, *What is Technology?* and *How does Society Decide?* SATIS 8–14, the most recent SATIS initiative, provides activities for upper primary and lower secondary school pupils.

Science with Technology Project

Project Director: Jim Sage, 23 Westfield Park, Redland, Bristol BS6 6LT. Telephone: 0272 238943.

The project is a joint initiative of the Association for Science Education and the Design and Technology Association. Its aim is to develop the relationship between science and technology for students aged 14–19. The curriculum materials produced will become part of the ASE SATIS publications.

Technology Enhancement Programme

National Co-ordinator: John Holman; Module Team Leader: Jim Sage; details from Programme Manager: Sue Kearney, 20 Canon Street, Taunton, Somerset TA1 1SW. Telephone: 0823 323363.

The programme aims to enhance the delivery of technology, mathematics and science to students in the 14–19 age range. The modules produced are intended to support a range of routes to accreditation including GCSE, BTEC, City and Guilds, A/AS level and GNVQ. Amongst key principles of the programme are: that mathematics and science activities must be embedded into all TEP modules; and the modules are to be developed by teams of teachers of mathematics, science and technology working with advisers from industry.

The programme is funded by the Gatsby Charitable Foundation and managed by the Engineering Council. It has close links with the Science and Technology Project.

Nuffield Design and Technology Project

Project Directors: Dr David Barlex, Professor Paul Black and Professor Geoffrey Harrison, The Nuffield Chelsea Curriculum Trust, King's College London, 552 King's Road, London SW10 0UA.

The Nuffield Chelsea Curriculum Trust and Longman Education are supporting a curriculum development project for design and technology at Key Stages 3 and 4 (students aged 11–16 years). It is intended that those who follow a course based on the project's materials will develop a technical understanding of the mathematics and science required to solve technological problems, skill in making, competence in the strategies of design and technology, a sensitivity to the needs of people and the environment, and creativity in devising solutions to meet these needs (*Newsletter 2*).

Technology in Context

The Technology in Context Programme, Standing Conference on Schools' Science and Technology, 76 Portland Place, London W1N 4AA. Telephone: 071 278 2468.

Curriculum materials are part of an integrated support service for schools provided by the project, the prime aim of which is to help pupils display progressive ability to apply business concepts and knowledge to the process of designing and making. The project supports technology education and the cross-curricular theme of economic and industrial understanding. Several of the resource packs incorporate the use of scientific knowledge and skills in industrial contexts.

CREST (CREativity in Science and Technology)

Director: Alan West, CREST Award Scheme, Education Liaison Centre, University of Surrey, Guildford GU22 5XH.

This scheme is sponsored by the Department for Education, and by industry, and is supported jointly by the British Association for the Advancement of Science and the Standing Conference on Schools' Science and Technology. Its primary aim is to support scientific and technological problem solving by students in the 11–18 age range. It complements normal school work and is non-competitive, students gaining recognition for their work by a series of awards (bronze, silver or gold) each of which is criterion referenced.

References

Barlex, D. (1991) Using science in design and technology. *Design and Technology Teaching*, 23(3), 148–51.

Carlson, W.B. and Gorman, M.E. (1990) Understanding invention as a cognitive process. The case of Thomas Edison and early motion pictures, 1888–91. *Social Studies of Science*, 20, 387–430.

French, M.J. (1988) *Invention and Evolution. Design in Nature and Engineering*. Cambridge, Cambridge University Press.

Gorman, M.E. and Carlson, W.B. (1990) Interpreting invention as a cognitive process: the case of Alexander Graham Bell, Thomas Edison and the telephone. *Science, Technology and Human Values*, 15(2), 131–64.

Nuffield Design and Technology Initiative (1992) *Newsletter 2*. Nuffield Chelsea Curriculum Trust and Longman Education.

Rankine, W.J.M. (1857) *The Science of Engineering*. London, Griffin.

Secretary of State for Education and Secretary of State for Wales (1992) *Technology for Ages 5 to 16 (1992)*. Proposals of the Secretary of State for Education and the Secretary of State for Wales. London, Department for Education and Welsh Office.

Young, M. and Barnett, M. (1992) *The Technological Baccalaureate. An Interim Evaluation of the Pilot Project prepared by the Post-16 Education Centre in Conjunction with the Technology and Education Unit*. London, Institute of Education, University of London.

Index

abstraction, level of, 58
academic knowledge, 12, 15
AC induction motor, 54
Advisory Council for Applied Research and Development (ACARD), 41–2
aeroplane design, 39
Aikenhead, G., 22
Aitken, H. J. G., 24, 49, 51
American Association for the Advancement of Sciences, 42
applied science, 41, 42
APU model of interaction between mind and hand, 37
APU science problem-solving model, 46
artefactual discontinuity, 39
ASE Policy Statement on Technology, 76–7
Association for Science Education, 20, 46, 60, 61, 62, 64, 72
attainment targets, 20–1, 23, 38–9, 61
Australia, 14
automobile, how it has altered our lives, 34

Bangladesh, 29
Barlex, D., 75
basic research, 25
bearings, 45
Black, Maggie, 29
Blackett, P. M. S., 25
Botswana, 64
breathalyser, 22
British Association for the Advancement of Science, 78
Bush, Vannevar, 25

CAD-CAM, 14
capability tasks, 75–6
Carnot, Sadi, 51–3
CDT, 18–19, 20
cellulase, 71–2
cellulose, 71–2
Clerk Maxwell, J., 24, 54
cognitive process models, 36–7
computer education, 14
computers and women, 35
consumer–contractor principle, 41
contextualisation, 59
Council of Industrial Design, 18
CNC, 14
craft subjects, 17
CREST (Creativity in Science and Technology), 78
critic competence, 61
curriculum organisation, 57

DDT, 33
De Forest, Lee, 24
Department for Education, 78
design, 15, 17–18
  parameters, 49, 51, 76
  repertoire, 75
design and technology
  capability, 61
  models of, 36–9
Design and Technology Assocation, 72
design and technology in the National Curriculum of England and Wales, 20–2, 46–7, 61
Design Council, 18
designer molecules, 49
developing countries, 64
De Vries, Marc, 37

Edison, Thomas, 26
education, economic influences on, 11–12
Education Reform Act 1988, 17
electronics, 18, 62, 63
empirical inquiry, 43
energy, 18
England and Wales, 14, 17, 20, 38, 57, 60
entitlement, 77
environmental education, 64
essential science, 73
excreta-related diseases, 49–51

faults, diagnosing and rectifying, 61
Fensham, Peter, 62
Finland, 11, 14
Fleming, J. Ambrose, 24
food manufacturing, 11, 45
Forward Looking Infra-Red (FLIR) System, 49
French, M. J., 75

GCSE, 18
gender and technology, 33–6
Gandhi, M., 36
Giedion, Sigfried, 23
Goonatilake, Susantha, 31–2
great egg race, 67–9
green revolution, 32

handpumps, 28–9
Henry's Law, 28
Her Majesty's Inspectorate, 18, 20
hidden curriculum, 59–60
Hughes, Thomas, 26
Hynes, Patricia, 33, 35

India, 28–9
induction motor, 54
Industrial Arts Association, 13
information technology, 60
infra-red radiation, 49
Institute of Physics, 45
interactive design cycle, 36, 47
International Technology Education Association, 13
Ireland, 14

jeans, 70–2
Joseph, Sir Keith, 19

Keller, Alexander, 26
Kline, Stephen Jay, 27–8
Knamiller, Gary, 63
knowledge
  action knowledge, 12
  propositional knowledge, 12
Kuhn, Thomas, 39

Lapland, 31
Law, John, 32
laws of nature, 41
Lewis, John, 63

maker competence, 61
Malawi, 63
Marconi, Giuseppe, 24
Maxwellian electromagnetic theory, 54
mission-oriented research, 25
modelling, 69
monitoring competence, 61
Mumford, Lewis, 22, 24
MUST Project, 70–1, 72, 77

National Curriculum (England and Wales), 17, 20, 38, 60
National Energy Foundation's National Home Energy Rating, 53
National Science Foundation, 25
Netherlands, technology in, 13–14, 37, 38
Newcomen engine, 44, 51
Nigeria, 29
Noble, David, 31, 32
non-destructive testing, 45
normal
  science, 39
  technology, 39
Northern Foods plc, 45
Nuffield Advanced Physics Project, 63
Nuffield Design and Technology Project, 75, 75–6, 78
Nuffield Foundation Science Teaching Project, 19
nuclear magnetic resonance imaging, 49

operacy, 63
operational principles, 39, 48–9, 69, 69–70, 71
ozone layer, 33

Pacey, Arnold, 26–7, 28, 29, 37
paradigmatic competence, 61
patent law, 49
PCBs, 44
Perkin, William Henry, 24
Philippines, 64
philosophy of technology, 23
Polanyi, Michael, 48–9
Popper, Karl, 23, 64
problem-solving processes, 46, 62
Project Hindsight, 25
Project TRACES, 25
Project Technology, 18
Project 2061, 42
propositional knowledge, 12
pumps, village hand, 28–9
pure science, 42

quality assurance and control, 44–5

Rankine, W. J. M., 76
reconstruction of knowledge, 59
reindeer herding, 32
resource tasks, 75
revolutionary science, 39
Rosenberg, Nathan, 24–5
Rothschild, Lord, 41

Salters' Science/Chemistry, 42–3
SATIS Project, 69, 72, 77
Schön, Donald, 12
school and work, 12
school technology, 36–9
science
  for action, 19
  and/for applications, 22
  for citizens, 19
  curriculum, 18
  relations with technology, 25–6
  for scientists, 19
  and/with technology, 22, 42–3
Science with Technology Project, 72–4, 77
scientific knowledge, 49
Scotland, 14
Secondary Science Curriculum Review, 46–7
Smeaton, John, 44
Smiles, Samuel, 23, 33
snowmobile, 31–2
Society for the History of Technology, 23
Spain, 14
Standing Conference on Schools' Science and Technology, 78
Statutory Order for Technology 1990, 17, 20–1, 36–7
Staudenmaier, John, 51, 53
Steinmetz, Charles P., 54
strategic science, 42
structures, 18
STS, 19, 43, 62
sucralose, 49
systematic empirical inquiry, 43–4

technological
  awareness, 60, 61, 62
  Baccalaureate, 74
  change, 12
  determinism, 33
  knowledge, 49, 51–3, 54
  literacy, 60, 62, 77
  traditions, 39
technology
  across the curriculum, 59–62
  as artefact, 26
  assessment, 33
  combined with science, 62–4
  and external criteria, 48
  and gender, 33–6
  generic/enabling technologies, 42
  and household work, 35–6
  and human work, 35
  in the National Curriculum of England and Wales, 17, 20–1, 38–9
  nature of, 26–9
  neutrality of, 31
  normal and revolutionary, 39
  not applied science, 24–5
  origins of school technology, 13–15
  relationship with science, 25–6
  school technology, 36–9
  as a separate subject, 57–9
  as a social gene, 35
  as system, 26–9
  as a third culture, 13
  transfer of, 31–2
  unintended outcomes of, 33
  and values, 13, 21, 31–3
  in vocational education, 15
Technology Enhancement Programme, 77
Technology in Context Programme, 78
technology-oriented science syllabuses, 63
Thatcher, Margaret, 18, 41
thermodynamics, 53
thought-in-action, 36
tungsten-halogen lamps, 44
TVEI, 11

values, 13, 21, 31–3
vocationalism, 11, 12, 13

UNICEF's rural water supply and sanitation programme, 28–9
USA, technology in, 11, 13, 28, 43, 45, 54, 65
useful science, 73
user competence, 61
Usher, A. P., 23

water-related diseases, 49–51
water, rural supply of, 28–9
Watt, James, 51
Wigglesworth, V. B., 47–8
women and technology, 33–6

Zimbabwe, 11, 63